Happily Ever After

Studies in the Beatitudes

by
Jeff Cranston

Published by
John Broadbanks Publishing

Published by John Broadbanks Publishing

F. W. Boreham

Lover of Life: F. W. Boreham's Tribute to His Mentor (Revised and Expanded)
All the Blessings of Life: The Best Stories of F. W. Boreham (Revised)
Second Thoughts
The Chalice of Life: Reflections on the Significant Stages in Life
A Packet of Surprises: The Best Essays and Sermons of F. W. Boreham
Angels, Palms and Fragrant Flowers: F. W. Boreham on C. H. Spurgeon
Loose Leaves

Geoff Pound

Making Life Decisions: Journey in Discernment

Jeff Cranston

Happily Ever After: Studies in the Beatitudes

John Broadbanks Publishing
Eureka, CA
2010

10 9 8 7 6 5 4 3

Printed in the United States of America

ISBN-13 978-0-9790334-9-0
ISBN-10 0-9790334-9-7

Cover Design: Laura Zugzda
Interior Layout: ADI and Stephanie Martindale

Table of Contents

This book is dedicated to
my wife, Darlene,
who consistently lives out the principles
of the Beatitudes,
and
the men and women
of LowCountry Community Church.
It's an awesome experience
living out the kingdom principles of God
with each one of you.

Acknowledgments

I'd like to say thank you to ...
Mom and Dad;
My wife Darlene, who shares her life with mine;
My daughters and son-in-law: Tiffany and Bryan, Lauren,
and Emily;
Pat Calhoun, for the editorial lay-outs;
Deborah Thorn, for her tireless efforts in checking style
and grammar;
Hannah Thorn, for creating the study and discussion questions;
Jimmy Taylor, for pushing this project through to completion;
My friends at John Broadbanks Publishing:
Michael Dalton and Geoff Pound;
John and Sandi Reed, who provided me with an inspirational
location in which to scribble these thoughts; and,
My ministry colleagues at LowCountry Community Church
who make serving God as part of a team all I dreamed it could be.

By Way Of Introduction

What a delight it has been to spend time with the teachings of Jesus Christ through the "Beatitudes." I feel as if, after spending hundreds of hours in reading, preparation, and writing, I am only scratching the surface. I join a host of other writers who have felt the same frustration—one, however, borne out of gratefulness—that no one is able to plumb the depths of the truths presented in Scripture.

In his book, *Dreams at Sunset,* author F. W. Boreham recounts a story from early American history. "It was a sultry day; the little meeting house was crowded; and, to render conditions more tolerable, the doors and windows stood wide open. Whilst the meeting was in progress, the red men emerged silently from the woods and crept like snakes across the open space that surrounded the building. Their chief, the terrible Black Eagle, was at their head. Gliding toward the open door, he was determined to observe the disposition of those within, and at the right moment, to give the signal for the impending massacre. But, as he paused beside the portal, he heard a voice—subdued, reverent, and stately—reading some strange and wondrous words. The sentences to which he listened with astonishment were these:

Blessed are the poor in spirit:
for theirs is the kingdom of heaven.
Blessed are they that mourn: for they shall be comforted.
Blessed are the meek: for they shall inherit the earth.
Blessed are they which do hunger and thirst after
righteousness: for they shall be filled ...

... and so on.

"As stealthily as he had come, Black Eagle crept away. 'If these be the laws of the white men,' he said, 'let them live and teach the red men the same holy doctrine!'"

Black Eagle recognized that the Beatitudes ennoble in us a character which is borne of rock-solid faith. May his heart cry as he heard the words of Scripture through the open portal be ours as well.

— Jeff Cranston

East Fork Ranch
Cruso, North Carolina
Easter, 2010

Beatitudes

Now when he saw the crowds, he went up on a mountainside and sat down. His disciples came to him, and he began to teach them saying:

"Blessed are the poor in spirit,
   for theirs is the kingdom of heaven.
Blessed are those who mourn,
   for they will be comforted.
Blessed are the meek,
   for they will inherit the earth.
Blessed are those who hunger and thirst for righteousness,
   for they will be filled.
Blessed are the merciful,
   for they will be shown mercy.
Blessed are the pure in heart,
   for they will see God.
Blessed are the peacemakers,
   for they will be called sons of God.
Blessed are those who are persecuted because of righteousness,
   for theirs is the kingdom of heaven.
Blessed are you when people insult you, persecute you and
   falsely say all kinds of evil against you because of me. Rejoice
   and be glad, because great is your reward in heaven, for in the
   same way they persecuted the prophets who were before you."

— Matthew 5:1-12, NIV

It appears to me that too many Christians want to enjoy the thrill of feeling right but are not willing to endure the inconvenience of being right. And so, the divorce between theory and practice becomes permanent in fact. Truth sits forsaken and grieves till her professed followers come home for a brief visit. But she sees them depart again when the bills come due.

— A. W. Tozer

CHAPTER ONE

Hearing His Voice Today

In a classic comic, Calvin and Hobbes are talking about the new year when Calvin says, *"I'm getting disillusioned with these new years. They don't seem very new at all. Each new year is just like the old year. Here another year has gone by and everything's still the same. There's still pollution and war and stupidity and greed.... I thought things were supposed to improve. I thought the future was supposed to be better."* After listening to this skeptical soliloquy, Hobbes replies, *"The problem with the future is that it keeps turning into the present."*

Do you ever feel that way? While it's difficult to put the past behind us, it's even more challenging to be proactive in the present so that we're transformed tomorrow. And some of us make resolutions in the New Year in the hopes that the future won't turn into the present. I came across a list of the "Top Ten New Year's Resolutions." Not surprisingly, the top four were health-related, but two of the ten dealt with the health of the soul:

Top Ten New Year's Resolutions

1. Lose Weight
2. Exercise
3. Quit Smoking
4. Quit Drinking
5. Be A Better Person
6. Spend More Time With The Family
7. Spend Less Time On The Internet

8. Be More Organized

9. Get Out Of Debt

10. Be More Spiritual

We want things to be different in a new year, but we quickly find out how elusive real change can be.

I recently came across the following true story: At the beginning of a new year, a high school principal decided to post his teachers' New Year's resolutions on the bulletin board. As the teachers gathered around the bulletin board, a great commotion started. One of the teachers was complaining. *"Why weren't my resolutions posted?"* She was throwing such a temper tantrum that the principal hurried to his office to see if he had overlooked her resolutions. Sure enough, he had mislaid them on his desk. As he read her resolutions he was astounded. This teacher's first resolution was not to let little things upset her in the new year.

We wish each other "Happy New Year" without really thinking through what that means. Is there a way to be happy, or is there more to life than the pursuit of happiness? How can we become better people? I'd like to suggest that we must develop a disciple's attitude in order to have not only a happy New Year annually but in order to live a holy life. Happiness and joy come from hearing God's voice to us and obeying His commands, precepts, and calls.

It could have been a day much like today when the Greatest Teacher who ever lived preached the greatest sermon ever preached. That teacher, of course, is the Lord Jesus, and the sermon is called the Sermon on the Mount. Matthew tells us, "And when He saw the multitudes, He went up on the mountain; and after He sat down, His disciples came to Him. And opening His mouth He began to teach them." [1]

On that day He saw the multitudes of people who needed to hear a fresh word from God. They, like many today, were hungry for something which would speak life to their hearts. Tired of the opinions of people and the abstract theological ramblings of the religious leaders of the day, they wanted a relevant message they could apply to their lives. And that would be what they would get.

As we prepare to reflect on the words of Jesus' great sermon in this book—words that are full of power, wisdom, insight, love, grace, and life—we must recognize that it is possible to hear the greatest sermon ever spoken and go away unchanged by it. Unless the ground is prepared to receive the seed, the seed will never penetrate that ground and, consequently, will never take root and eventually die.

What can we do to make sure that we hear His voice today and receive the full benefit of the most powerful Word spoken to the human race? Perhaps a passage from the book of James would assist us in examining our ability to receive God's Word into our lives.

"But let everyone be quick to hear, slow to speak and slow to anger; for the anger of man does not achieve the righteousness of God. Therefore putting aside all filthiness and all that remains of wickedness, in humility receive the word implanted, which is able to save your souls. But prove yourselves doers of the word, and not merely hearers who delude themselves. For if anyone is a hearer of the word and not a doer, he is like a man who looks at his natural face in a mirror; for once he has looked at himself and gone away, he has immediately forgotten what kind of person he was."[2]

As we read those words, let's ask ourselves this question and see if we can grasp a couple of answers: *"How do we properly and adequately receive the Word of God into our lives?"*

An Attentive Heart

Cultivate an attentive heart

We must be quick to hear the Word of truth. "Quick to hear" refers to an *alert* ear. It is possible to hear and yet not listen. We do that all the time when we speak with one another; we hear without listening to what the other person is saying. James is not talking about physically hearing the words as they impact our ears, but *listening* for what God has to say. "Quick to hear" describes an attentive heart—listening for what God has to say.

Often we talk to one another and never really hear what the other person has to say. When we ask someone, "How are you doing?" and they give us any other answer besides, "I'm doing fine," (the only one we're programmed to hear) we may miss it altogether. We are not programmed to hear different kinds of answers. We are not quick to hear when it comes to receiving what others are trying to tell us. That is often true when it comes to what God is trying to communicate to us. That's why Jesus was always talking about "having ears to hear."

One of my favorite stories regarding this is shared by my friend, Dr. Bill Boerop. It regards his granddaughter, Lindsay. She was called for dinner three times by her mom, Gloria. "Lindsay, it's time for supper. Please come in now." After receiving no response, Gloria said it one more time. Finally, Lindsay responded by saying, "Mommy, I'm not obeying *because I can't hear you!*"

In one Gospel, it says, *"Take heed **what** you hear;"* in another Gospel it says, *"Take heed **how** you hear."* We not only have to concentrate on the facts, we have to concentrate on the attitude of our heart in hearing the facts. How does an attentive heart help me hear and apply the Word of God?

An attentive heart leads me to be slow to speak.

One of the things that keeps us from hearing is that we need to be—but are not—slow to speak. One of the reasons we don't listen is because we're doing all the talking! God gave us two ears and one mouth—that ought to say something to us. Many times we need to be quiet and let God speak to us.

The story is told of a young man who came to the philosopher, Socrates, to be instructed in oratory. When the young man was introduced, he began to talk incessantly. This went on for some time; and finally Socrates put his hand over the mouth of his young charge and said, "Young man, I'll have to charge you a double fee." The young man asked, "Why?" Socrates replied, "Because I have to teach you two lessons. One, the science of holding your tongue, and two, the science of using it correctly."

Sometimes we just need to shut up if we are going to hear God. We need to develop an attentive ear.

An attentive heart helps cultivate a calm spirit.

James cautions, "for the anger of man does not achieve the righteousness of God."[3] We need to cultivate a calm spirit. We need to be slow to anger. Did you know that being upset with what you hear can block all the capacity you possess to hear it, especially when it comes to a relevant word from God? If you don't calm your spirit down and let God speak a word to you, even when that word is uncomfortable, you will never hear. Cultivate a calm spirit.

An attentive heart leads to a clean heart.

James continues: *"Therefore putting aside all filthiness and all that remains of wickedness ..."*[4]

We also need to cultivate a clean heart. James exhorts us to continue putting aside all filthiness. This term, *filthiness* or *moral filth*, comes from a root word in Greek that has to do with earwax; but James is referring to sin. In other words, sin in your life is like earwax—it will prevent you from hearing God. It stops up the capacity to hear. The Bible teaches that sin separates our hearts from God's. Isaiah said, *"The Lord GOD has opened My ear."*[5] God sometimes has to dig our ears out so that we can hear what He has to say. If you listen for God to speak, you will hear His voice.

A Teachable Spirit

James continues, *"...in humility receive the word implanted, which is able to save your souls."*[6] How does a teachable spirit receive the Word?

There are several keys here.

We receive it in humility.

Anger contributes to a spirit of arrogance. We don't want to hear what God has to say because we don't like it. We need to develop a teachable spirit if we are going to hear what God wants to communicate to us through His Word. Humility is spoken of in the fifth chapter of Galatians as one of the fruits of the Spirit. Jesus refers to humility in the Beatitudes, one of the eight attributes that characterize a Christian's walk and life (which we will examine in chapter four). Humility is essential to hearing the Word and receiving it.

The well-known 19th century preacher, Charles Spurgeon, defined humility as, "making a right estimate of one's self." Another noted speaker stated that, "Humility is not denying the power or gifting you have, but admitting that the gifting is from God and the power comes through you and not from you." After World War II, Winston Churchill humbly commented, "I was not the lion, but it fell to me to give the lion's roar."

I have followed the Lord for years now and find that the more I know about Jesus, the more there is to know—and need to know. I have only scratched the surface in my understanding about the things of God. If I am to press on and understand the things of God better, I must maintain a teachable spirit, or I will stay stuck in the mud in my spiritual walk. None of us have arrived. Paul said that he hadn't arrived; and if he hadn't, I can't think of anyone else who has. Paul said, *"Not that I have already obtained it, or have already become perfect, but I press on in order that I may lay hold of that for which also I was laid hold of by Christ Jesus."*[7] We need to develop a teachable heart and an open, receptive spirit.

The saints of God sometimes need to throw off all they *think* they know. Often we have to unlearn some things to be taught again. The idea of receiving the Word has a connotation in the original language of showing hospitality. This word is used for how we receive others into our homes. Here it is used for how we receive the Word of God into our lives. It's not just enough to hear the Word; we have to welcome it. The welcoming of the Word takes place when we are humble enough and teachable enough for God to speak to us. In other words, we are to give God's Word a warm welcome. Receive the Word of God into your life. Obey it and it will accomplish its work.

An Obedient Walk

"But prove yourselves doers of the word, and not merely hearers who delude themselves."[8]

Many Christians stop at merely hearing and receiving the Word. They hear the Word and receive it but don't take the essential step to do what the Word commands. Let's illustrate it from something Chuck Swindoll writes in his book, *Improving Your Serve:*

"To make the value of obedience just as practical as possible, let's play 'Let's Pretend.' Let's pretend that you work for me. In fact, you are my executive assistant in a company that is growing rapidly. I'm the owner and I'm interested in expanding overseas. To pull this off, I make plans to travel abroad and stay there until a new branch office gets established. I make all the arrangements to take my family and move to Europe for six to eight months. And I leave you in charge of the busy state side organization. I tell you that I will write you regularly and give you directions and instructions. I leave and you stay. Months pass. A flow of letters are mailed from Europe and received by you at the national headquarters. I spell out all my expectations. Finally, I return. Soon after my arrival, I drive down to the

office and I am stunned. Grass and weeds have grown up high. A few windows along the street are broken. I walk into the Receptionist's room. She is doing her nails, chewing gum and listening to her favorite radio station. I look around and notice the wastebaskets are overflowing. The carpet hasn't been vacuumed for weeks, and nobody seems concerned that the owner has returned. I asked about your whereabouts and someone in the crowded lounge area points down the hall and yells, 'I think he's down there.' Disturbed, I move in that direction and bump into you as you are finishing a chess game with our sales manager. I ask you to step into my office, which has been temporarily turned into a television room for watching afternoon soap operas. 'What in the world is going on, man?'

'What do you mean, Chuck?'

'Well, look at this place! Didn't you get any of my letters?'

'Letters? Oh yes! Sure! I got every one of them. As a matter of fact, Chuck, we have had a letter study every Friday night since you left. We have even divided the personnel into small groups to discuss many of the things you wrote. Some of the things were really interesting. You will be pleased to know that a few of us have actually committed to memory some of your sentences and paragraphs. One or two memorized an entire letter or two—great stuff in those letters.'

'Okay. You got my letters. You studied them and meditated on them; discussed and even memorized them. But what did you do about them?'

'Do? We didn't do anything about them.'"[9]

This fictitious story loses all its tongue-in-cheek humor when we consider the unhappy fact that this fictional situation well-describes many of our churches and 21st century Christians.

Sometimes our actions and attitudes even reinforce this mentality. We encourage our children to memorize Scripture and reward them for the mere fact of Scripture memorization without the consequent obedience to that Scripture. Jeremy Kingsley, noted speaker to today's youth says, "Don't read God's Word to finish; read God's Word to change." You see, God gives us His Word, not to make us smart, but so that we will obey it. God says through James, *"But prove yourselves doers of the word, and not merely hearers who delude themselves."*[10] Sometimes we hear and receive the Word; we memorize it; we can tell people the facts and the truths of the Word of God; yet, we do not live that same Word out. If we are merely hearers, we delude ourselves.

James continues with an illustration: *"For if anyone is a hearer of the word and not a doer, he is like a man who looks at his natural face in a mirror; for once he has looked at himself and gone away, he has immediately forgotten what kind of person he was."*[11]

James compares the Word of God to a mirror. The mirror shows us what we really look like. Most of the time when we look into the mirror, we do it for other reasons besides seeing ourselves. Sometimes we look into the mirror to shave or put on makeup. Many times you can go through that routine without ever seeing what you look like. But if you do study that image, you will see an accurate reflection of who you are.

The Word of God is like that. When you look into the Word of God and hear His truth, you see who you really are as you compare your choices and heart to the truth of God's Word. The Word of God, like a mirror, reveals to us who we really are.

If we just hear the Word, we are like somebody who glances in the mirror and shaves his face, or applies her lipstick, and walks away and doesn't really remember what they look like. I have this idealized image of myself. I think I am still the good-looking guy (!) I was twenty years ago. But the mirror pops my bubble. Most of us probably think we look differently than we really do.

When I was a young boy, I recall visiting my uncle David. His body was crippled by muscular dystrophy, and he spent many years of his life in a wheelchair. He was only a few years older than I and a huge fan of the British pop group, The Beatles. David had a reel-to-reel tape recorder and player. One night, he had me speak into a microphone and recorded my voice. I'll never forget the first time I ever heard the sound of my own voice! I couldn't believe it was me. You may recall when you heard your recorded voice for the first time. You said, "I don't sound like that!" But you do. The tape is precisely how you sound. Someone views a home video and exclaims, "I don't look like that!" Yes, you do! That's precisely how you look. We have an idea of what we really want to be and what we want to look like. Sometimes that's true in our Christian lives. We deceive ourselves into believing we are something we are not simply because we know the facts of the Word of God. A. W. Tozer put it well when he wrote:

"There is an evil which, in its effect on the Christian religion, may be more destructive than communism, Romanism, and liberalism combined. It is the glaring disparity between theology and practice among professing Christians. So wide is this gulf between theory and practice in the church that an inquiring stranger who chances upon both, would scarcely dream that there was any relation between the two of them. An intelligent observer of our human scene who heard the Sunday morning message and later watched the Sunday afternoon conduct of those who heard it would conclude that he had been examining two distinct and contrary religions. It appears to me that too many Christians want to enjoy the thrill of feeling right but are not willing to endure the inconvenience of being right. And so, the divorce between theory and practice becomes permanent in fact. Truth sits forsaken and grieves till her

professed followers come home for a brief visit. But she sees them depart again when the bills come due.[12]

When we fail to obey the Word, there is a disparity between what we profess and what we possess; what we say we believe and what we actually believe; who we say we are and who we really are. Jesus has not called us to become people who know the Word only. He has called us to be people who live the Word, who obey the Word. How do you do that? You do it by "doing." Simply do it! Obey it! Live it! Make it your daily habit to spend time with God in His Word. Challenge yourself to make a choice each day to allow the Word to change your habits into God's character.

I am your constant companion. I am your greatest helper or heaviest burden. I will push you onward or drag you down to failure. I am completely at your command. Half of the things you do you might just as well turn over to me and I will be able to do them quickly and correctly. I am easily managed—you must merely be firm with me. Show me exactly how you want something done, and after a few lessons I will do it automatically.

I am the servant of all great men; and alas, of all failures as well. Those who are great, I have made great. Those who are failures, I have made failures. I am not a machine, though I work with all the precision of a machine plus the intelligence of a man. You may run me for profit or run me for ruin—it makes no difference to me. Take me, train me, be firm with me, and I will place the world at your feet. Be easy with me and I will destroy you.

Who am I? I am habit! [13]

Make it your daily habit, not only to read and hear the Word of God, but to obey it in every aspect of your life.

How do we receive the Word? We need to develop an attentive heart to hear the Word of God. We need to develop a teachable spirit to receive the Word of God. Finally, we need to develop an obedient walk to obey the Word of God. If you do this, the Bible says that you will be blessed.

If you are going to be changed by the teachings of Jesus Christ found in the Beatitudes, these qualities will need to be in you. Are they? Are you listening with your spiritual ears to what God wants to tell you? Do you have a teachable spirit open to what God has to say, or is your theology too closed and narrow to hear a fresh word? When God speaks, are you willing to do what He says? If you are willing to hear and obey, God will gladly tell you the next step to take. May God give you the grace to take it.

Let's end this chapter with one final sentence from James: *"But one who looks intently at the perfect law, the law of liberty, and abides by it, not having become a forgetful hearer but an effectual doer, this man shall be blessed in what he does."* [14]

The world has its own idea of blessedness. Blessed is the man who is always right. Blessed is the man who is satisfied with himself. Blessed is the man who is strong. Blessed is the man who rules. Blessed is the man who is popular. Blessed is the man who enjoys life. These are the beatitudes of sight and the present world. It comes with a shock and opens a new realm of thought that not one of these men entered Jesus' mind when he treated of blessedness.

—*Ian Maclaren*

❖

CHAPTER TWO

The Attitude of Reception

"Blessed are the poor in spirit, for
theirs is the kingdom of heaven."
Matthew 5:3

In his book, *The Body*, author and former Watergate conspirator-turned-Christian, Charles Colson, relates that at the height of her fame as the other woman in the Ivana and Donald Trump breakup, Marla Maples spoke of her religious roots. She believed in the Bible, she told interviewers, then added the disclaimer, *"but you can't always take [it] literally and be happy."*[1]

Jesus never stated that following His precepts would bring worldly happiness; He told us that following His teaching would bring blessing.

Christ begins His sermon with blessings, for *"He came into the world to bless us,*[2] and it is through Him that ... *all the families of the earth should be blessed."*[3] He came not only to purchase blessings for us but to pour out and pronounce blessings on us; and in Matthew five, Jesus does this as one having authority; as one that can command the blessing. Just think: those whom the Lord chooses to bless are indeed blessed!

The Old Testament ended with a threatened curse: *"He will turn the hearts of the fathers to their children, and the hearts of the children to their fathers; or else I will come and strike the land with a curse."*[4] The New Testament, however, begins with blessings!

All eight of the characteristics in the "Beatitudes" that we should display in our lives are introduced with the word, "blessed." God wants to give His approval to those who put Him first.

I once heard of a family that went to the state park for a day to enjoy the great outdoors. When they arrived, they saw a whole row of signs that said, *"No hunting! No fishing! No camping! No picnicking! No trespassing! No hiking!"* At the bottom of another sign, in small print, the family read, *"This is your state park; enjoy it!"* In this sermon, Jesus is giving us not a list of "don'ts" but a list of "do's." They are really "Be-attitudes" because this is how we should be in our attitudes and actions.

As He begins the "Sermon on the Mount," Jesus gives us eight characteristics of blessed people which represent to us the principles of grace in the Christian life. Each "Beatitude" contains a blessing that can be attained both now and in the future.

The Benefits of Blessing

Why does God choose to bless His people? Blessedness enables us to have a true view of life. Blessings are designed to rectify the ruinous mistakes of a blind and sinful world. A blessed life is what many people pretend to pursue: *"Many are asking, 'Who can show us any good?' Let the light of your face shine upon us, O Lord."* [5] Yet so many form a wrong notion of happiness; no wonder they miss the way. Bible commentator Matthew Henry writes, *"They choose their own delusions, and court a shadow."* [6]

The word Jesus uses for blessed means *blissful, fortunate,* or *happy.* In other words, Jesus is saying that this characteristic of being poor in spirit is one that will make us happy. But most people in our society today would argue the opposite. Many would argue that poverty of spirit leads to despair, not happiness. They would say, *"Happy are the successful, the powerful, the rich, the famous, the aggressive, the self-reliant, the self-confident, the glamorous."* Being poor in spirit is equated with being depressed, weak, timid, and passive. Everyone knows that this is not how you get ahead! This is not how you attain happiness! they say. A paraphrased philosophy of the famous atheist, Nietzsche, might well say, *"Assert yourself. Care for nothing except for yourself. The only vice is weakness, and the only virtue is strength. Be strong; be a superman. The world is yours if you can get it."*

This idea, tragically, has been baptized by many within the church. There are some preachers, teachers, and writers who pass this conventional wisdom as biblical teaching. They claim that following Jesus guarantees material prosperity, physical health, financial wealth, worldly success, and temporal happiness. This is not biblical Christianity. It does not have its eyes on the eternal. In this kind of "theology," God becomes the means to the end—a cosmic St. Nick. But God is more than a means to an end. Jesus had more in mind than temporal happiness. He is pointing us to the path of true happiness, and the place to begin is to become poor in spirit.

Most in our world today are of the following mind-set: Blessed are they that are rich, and great, and honored by the world; they spend their days satisfied, and their years in pleasure; they eat the best steaks at Ruth's Chris Steak House, drink the finest Bordeaux wine, and carry on in life with their heads held high. They have their business competitors bowing before them. Their designs and their aims in life, all lean toward the truth they have purchased with their souls: God (if there is one) will bless the covetous. Please don't think that this way of thinking is new to the 21st century.

The psalmist penned: *"For they brag about their evil desires; they praise the greedy and curse the Lord."*[7]

The Lord Jesus comes to the crowd that has gathered before Him and immediately begins to correct this fundamental error by advancing a new hypothesis. He gives us quite another notion of blessedness and blessed people; at first glance it appears to us to be paradoxical; it *can't* make sense! And yet as these verities begin to sink in, we realize it is a teaching of eternal truth by which we will one day be judged. If this, therefore, is the beginning of Christ's teaching and doctrine, the beginning of our lives as Christ followers must be to take our measures of happiness from those maxims of Jesus and to direct our life-long pursuits accordingly.

Blessedness not only helps us see life as it really is, blessedness also brings encouragement to our lives. Blessedness is designed to remove the discouragements we face when we feel weak and poor by assuring us that Christ's Gospel not only fulfills those whose lives are already seemingly blessed; but that even the least in the kingdom of heaven, whose hearts are right with God, can rejoice in the honors and privileges of His kingdom!

Blessedness is also God's desire for us. Imagine that in my hands is a white poster board. In the midst of all that whiteness, I make a large black dot in its center with a marking pen. If I were to then hold up the poster before a group of people and ask them what they see, how do you think they would respond? Here's how the conversation generally goes when I have done this in a group setting:

"What do you see?"

"I see a black circle."

"What else do you see?"

Silence.

"Did anyone here notice anything besides the black dot? Did anyone notice this large sheet of white poster board? You have completely overlooked the most important thing of all—the sheet of paper."

In life, we are often distracted by small, dot-like disappointments or painful experiences; and we are prone to forget the innumerable blessings we receive from the hand of the Lord. And like the sheet of white paper, the good things are far more important than the adversities that monopolize our attention. This reminds me of a bit of verse which, though I admit is somewhat trite, does express good practical advice. Someone has written:

"As you travel down life's pathway,
may this ever be your goal:
Keep your eye upon the doughnut,
and not upon the hole!"

Rather than concentrating on the trials of life, we should fix our attention upon its blessings. Let us say with the psalmist, *"Praise be to the Lord, to God our Savior, who daily bears our burdens."*[8]

Another benefit of God's blessing is that it brings joy into our lives. The teachings of Jesus are providentially designed to settle and summarize the points of agreement between God and man. This panorama of divine revelation is to let us know what God expects from us and what we may then expect from Him. No where is this more fully presented so succinctly than in the fifth chapter of Matthew. This is the Gospel which we embrace, for what is our faith but an outworking toward obtaining these characteristics, and a total reliance upon these promises of Christ? The doorway to fulfillment swings open wide, and we see set before us a broad, expansive highway. Isaiah writes, *"And a highway will be there; it will be called the Way of Holiness. The unclean will not journey on it; it will be for those who walk in that Way; wicked fools will not go about on it."*[9]

Everything that we receive in the way of blessings comes to us through the Lord Jesus Christ. Nothing passes between God and fallen man, except through Jesus. Others may have notions of how to gain God's blessings and favor; but if we are not looking toward the Savior, we will never experience them.

What It Means To Be Poor

We received the "Beatitudes" in the Greek language (it has since been translated into English by John Wycliffe in 1384). To adequately and fully understand these specific words of Christ, we need a grasp of what this idea of *poor* or *poverty* was to the Greek mind.

In the Greek language of the first-century, there are two words for *poor*. The first describes the person who has to work for a living; it's defined as the person who works with his or her hands to make a living. This person has often been referred to as the "working-man." My ancestors—six generations back on my father's side—worked as carpenters. They worked with their hands to scratch out a living. In Greek thought, the working man has nothing that is superfluous; they are not necessarily rich, but neither are they destitute. This is the person who has enough to get by and provide for his family, yet someone who has nothing extra.

But that's not the word Jesus used here in Matthew 5:3. The second Greek word describes absolute and abject poverty. It is connected to another word which means to *cower* or to *cover*; and it describes the poverty which is beaten to its knees. The first word describes the person who has nothing extra. The word Jesus chose to use, however, describes the person who has nothing at all. We may then rightly say, *Blessed is the man who is absolutely poverty-stricken. Blessed is the woman who is absolutely destitute.*

If you are a student of the Bible, you know that the "Beatitudes" were not originally spoken in Greek; Jesus spoke these words in Aramaic to a prominently Jewish audience. The Greeks had two key words they employed for *poor*; the Jews also had a special way of using the word *poor*.

In Hebrew the word for *poor* was developed through a sort of staging process; there is a evolution of its meaning. It looks something like this:

If I am poor, I therefore have no influence or power;
because I have no influence or power, I am oppressed;
because I am oppressed, I have no earthly resources whatsoever;
therefore,I must place all of my trust in God.

To the mind of Jesus' original hearers, the word *poor*, therefore, means the humble and helpless person who places his or her total trust in God.

This is exactly how the Psalmists use the word throughout the book of Psalms. Let's review just a few usages: *"This poor man called, and the Lord heard him; He saved him out of all his troubles."*[10] *"My whole being will exclaim, 'Who is like you, O Lord? You rescue the poor from those too strong for them, the poor and needy from those who rob them.'"*[11] *"Yet I am poor and needy; may the Lord think of me. You are my help and my deliverer; O my God, do not delay."*[12] *"The poor will see and be glad—you who seek God, may your hearts live!"*[13] *"Yet I am poor and needy; come quickly to me, O God. You are my help and my deliverer; O Lord, do not delay."*[14] *"I will bless her with abundant provisions; her poor will I satisfy with food."*[15]

Now, let's take the two usages of this phrase *poor in spirit* and place them together to gain a more complete understanding of what Jesus is teaching here. The Greek description portrays the person who is absolutely destitute, the person who has nothing at all; the Hebrew/Aramaic concept refers to the person who is poor, humble, and helpless, and has therefore, placed his or her whole trust in God. The Scottish commentator, William Barclay, combines these two ideas and paraphrases Matthew 5:3 like this: *"Blessed is the man who has realized his utter helplessness, and has put his trust in God."*

What This Means For The Follower Of Christ

If we are to totally reap the benefits of blessings from this beatitude, we must first acknowledge that we are born into an impoverished condition. *"Son of man, say to the leader of Tyre, 'Thus says the Lord God: Because your heart is lifted up and you have said,*

'I am a god, I sit in the seat of gods, in the heart of the seas'; Yet you are a man and not God, although you make your heart like the heart of God ...'[16]

Here we find a description of those who place themselves against God; who place themselves on the throne of their lives. Followers of Christ are to live lives opposite of this mindset.

This poverty in spirit is ranked first among the Christian graces. The Greek and Roman philosophers did not reckon humility to be paramount among their lists of moral virtues, but Christ puts it at the head of the list. Self-denial is the first lesson to be learned in His school. The foundation of all other graces is laid in humility. Those who build skyscrapers must begin deep in the ground with a solid and sure foundation. To build high, one must begin low. When I deny self and consider others as more important than I, I am preparing the soil of my heart for the entrance of the grace of Jesus to enter. Those *who are weary and heavy laden,* are the *poor in spirit,* and they shall find rest in Christ.

To be poor in spirit is to be the person who is afflicted and unable to save himself, looking therefore to God and only God for salvation, while recognizing that he has no claim on God. To be poor in spirit is to acknowledge my spiritual poverty, indeed my spiritual bankruptcy before God. It's acknowledging that I am a sinner, under the righteous and holy wrath of God, deserving nothing but punishment and banishment to hell because of my sin. I have nothing to offer God, nothing with which to plead my case, nothing with which I can purchase the favor of heaven.

A hymn-writer said it so well:

> *Nothing in my hand I bring,*
> *Simply to thy cross I cling;*
> *Naked, come to Thee for dress;*
> *Helpless, look to Thee for grace;*
> *Foul, I to the fountain fly;*
> *Wash me, Savior, or I die.*[17]

That's the language of the poor in spirit! We belong nowhere else except beside the tax collector in Jesus' parable. *"He would not even look up to heaven, but beat his breast and said, 'God, have mercy on me, a sinner.'"*[18] To such a person, and only to such a person, is given the kingdom of God.

This beatitude also reminds us that we must see our poverty against His plenty. The quickest way to become poor in spirit is to look at God. When we're in the presence of the One who is perfect, how can we boast about how good we are? God loves to bring us to the end of ourselves, to expose our deficiency so that we can see His sufficiency. We must be empty before we can be filled; and unless God fills us, we will forever remain empty. God's Word reminds us that His grace is sufficient for our every frailty (2 Corinthians 12:9); His wisdom is adequate for our every perplexity (James 1:5); His peace is ample for our every anxiety (Philippians 4:6-7); and His forgiveness is equal to every iniquity (1 John 1:9). God is enough!

God the Father has designed it so that salvation has been brought to us as a gift—an absolutely free gift—in the Person and work of the Lord Jesus Christ on the cross. We have to receive it with the dependence of a child.

When we reach this point spiritually before God, it is then He can pour out blessing upon blessing. We acknowledge our utter dependence upon Him, throwing ourselves upon the mercy and grace of the Lord Jesus. Then we can cry out, *"O, the joy of Christ! O, the bliss at being His! O, the joy of knowing Jesus Christ!"* All through Christ! All through Christ! All through Christ!

There Are Two Promises We Can Claim

That's not all! This beatitude comes with its accompanying promises. The first promise we may rightly claim is that we will be blessed, or approved by God, when we become poor in spirit. God is waiting to applaud those who admit their emptiness.

The second promise is this: The kingdom of heaven belongs to the children of God.

Not only the gospel message is given to and received by those who are poor in spirit, but all the benefits of the Gospel—its benevolence, bounty, care, and comfort—belongs to them. The poor in spirit hear the gospel message when it is preached to them; it not only reaches their ears, but their hearts—it enters into them. They receive it and embrace it with the utmost joy and gladness. Why? They know that eternal glory is being prepared for them. It is a gift from Christ Himself.

"For theirs is the kingdom of heaven." We can rightly say that the poor in spirit who inherit all of this from the gracious hand of their Heavenly Father are the congregation of the poor.

"O deliver not the soul of thy turtle dove unto the multitude of the wicked: forget not the congregation of thy poor for ever."[19] The kingdom of glory is prepared for them. Those who humble themselves and comply with God when He humbles them, shall be exalted. The spirits of today's world tag along with the glory of the kingdoms of the earth; but the humble, mild, and yielding followers of Jesus obtain the glory of the kingdom of heaven.

"For theirs is the kingdom of heaven." When we declare spiritual bankruptcy and depend on the provision of God's Son, He gives heaven to us as a free gift. We can experience a full and abundant life right now, with the assurance that we will spend eternity with Him when we die (see Ephesians 2:8-9).

Are you ready to admit your sinfulness and accept Jesus as your Substitute and Savior right now? If so, please pray this prayer from your heart.

> *Lord Jesus, for too long I've kept You out of my life. I admit that I am a sinner and that I cannot save myself. Please empty me of my arrogance. I repent of my sins by chang-ing my mind about the way I've been living. By faith I gratefully receive Your gift of salvation. Thank You, Lord Jesus, for coming to earth. With all my heart I believe You*

are the Son of God who died on the cross for my sins and rose from the dead on the third day. Thank You for bearing my sins and giving me the gift of eternal life. I believe Your words are true. I accept You into my heart. Be my Savior and Lord. I surrender to Your leadership in my life. Make me into the person You want me to be. Amen.

If you are already a follower of Jesus Christ, has a spiritual arrogance crept into your life lately? Have you failed to remember who you are before Almighty God? Then bow before Him and re-engage with your gracious Father through the words of the familiar hymn:

Nothing in my hand I bring,
Simply to Thy cross I cling;
Naked, come to Thee for dress;
Helpless, look to Thee for grace;
Foul, I to the fountain fly;
Wash me, Savior, or I die.

The Valley of Humiliation is the best and most fruitful stretch of country in all these parts. It is fertile ground, and, as you see, consisteth much in meadows. Behold how green the valley is; also how beautiful the lilies! And the pilgrims espied a boy keeping his father's sheep and singing the while, "He that is down needs fear no fall."

Then said their guide, "Do you hear him? I will dare to say that this boy lives a merrier life, and wears more of that herb called heartsease in his bosom, than he that is clad is silk and velvet."

And Mercy marveled at the effect of the valley upon her spirits. Nowhere else had she felt so well. She spoke of it to Mr. Greatheart, and his experience was akin to hers. "I have gone through this valley many a time," he said, "and never was better than when here." And he went on to say that most of the pilgrims whom he had escorted through the valley had said the same.

"I love to be in quiet places like this," Mercy added. "Methinks one may be here, without much molestation, be thinking what he was, whence he came, what he has done, and to what his King has called him. Here one may think and break at heart, and may melt in one's spirit until one's eyes become like the fish-pools of Heshbon."

—John Bunyan

❖

CHAPTER THREE

The Attitude of Mourning

"Blessed are those who mourn, for they will be comforted."
Matthew 5:4

Have you noticed that our culture embraces entertainment and pursues pleasure at all costs? Most of life is spent avoiding sorrow and pain. Even when we get bad news on TV, the newscasts often conclude with a funny story or something designed to make us smile. The mantra of many today is something like this: *"Blessed are those who laugh their way through life."* Some of us will do almost anything to stifle our sadness and turn away from tears. And yet, if we were honest, we'd have to admit that we sometimes feel like the writer of Proverbs when he said, *"Even in laughter the heart may ache, and joy may end in grief."*[1] The poet Robert Browning Hamilton said it well when he wrote,

"I walked a mile with Pleasure, she chatted all the way
But left me none the wiser for all she had to say.
I walked a mile with Sorrow and not a word said she,
But oh, the things I learned when sorrow walked with me."

In one of the most profound and paradoxical texts in the Bible, Jesus declares in Matthew 5:4: *"Blessed are those who mourn; for they will be comforted."* This startling contradiction could be put this way: *"Happy are the unhappy"* or *"The gladness of sadness"* or, *"God alongside of you when you're in agony."* This beatitude flows from the first one: *"Blessed are the poor in spirit; for theirs is the kingdom of heaven,"* because spiritual bankruptcy should always lead to spiritual brokenness. As John Stott says, "It is one thing to be spiritually poor and acknowledge it; it is another to grieve and to mourn over it ... confession is one thing, contrition is another."[2]

Of the different words that can be translated *mourn*, Jesus is using the strongest one available. It means to *grieve or wail*, as when a loved one dies. It is deep sorrow that causes the soul to ache and the heart to break. Jesus is not talking about complainers or whiners but about those who are gripped by grief.

I love the story about the great 19th century evangelist, D. L. Moody. While Moody was attending a convention in Indianapolis on mass evangelism, he asked his song leader, Ira Sankey, to meet him at six o'clock one evening at a certain street corner. When Sankey arrived, Mr. Moody asked him to stand on a box and sing. Once a crowd had gathered, Moody spoke briefly and then invited the people to follow him to the nearby convention hall. Soon the auditorium was filled with spiritually hungry people, and the great evangelist preached the Gospel to them.

Then the convention delegates began to arrive. Moody stopped preaching and said, "Now we must close, as the brethren of the convention wish to come and discuss the topic, 'How to reach the masses.'" Moody graphically illustrated the difference between talking about doing something and going out and doing it.

We can converse, pontificate and discuss this beatitude; but unless we draw some applications to our lives, we will miss the point Jesus wants us to grasp. I'd like to suggest four arenas in which this beatitude can be lived out in our lives.

Arena #1: Anguish Over Painful Experiences in Your Life

This first arena might be the easiest in that we all have experienced excruciating pain at some point in our lives; and if we haven't, we know it's coming. Peter writes, *"Dear friends, do not be surprised at the painful trial you are suffering, as though something strange were happening to you."*[3] You have possibly experienced, or are experiencing right now, some health issues that make you afraid about the future. Perhaps you've experienced a relational rupture with someone, and it's eating your heart out. Can you relate with the psalmist? *"I am worn out from groaning; all night long I flood my bed with weeping and drench my couch with tears."*[4]

Maybe you've lost a loved one through death, and you still cry yourself to sleep at night. You can relate to how David felt when his son Absalom died: *"The king was shaken. He went up to the room over the gateway and wept...."*[5] When Abraham's wife Sarah died, we read that he *"came to mourn ... and to weep for her."*[6]

Remember, that since Jesus wept when His friend Lazarus died, it's okay for you to cry as well. Solomon said in Ecclesiastes,

It is better to go to a house of mourning
than to go to a house of feasting,
because that is the end of every man,
and the living takes it to heart.
Sorrow is better than laughter,
for when a face is sad a heart may be happy.
The mind of the wise is in the house of mourning,
while the mind of fools is in the house of pleasure.[7]

In other words, it's better to attend a funeral than go to a party because sadness is actually good for us, especially if it helps prepare us for our own death and enable us to live like we should now.

Maybe you're weeping because you want to have a child, and you're still waiting. You know what it is to pine for the little child that never was. Your heart is breaking just like Hannah's did. *"In bitterness of soul Hannah wept much and prayed to the LORD.... 'I have been praying here out of my great anguish and grief.'"*[8]

Did you know that God collects every tear you shed? Psalm 56:8 relates, *"You number my wanderings. Put my tears into your bottle; are they not in your book?"*[9] Christianity is the only religion that allows you to be real. When you're hurting, express and release it. When you feel like crying, let the tears fall. God understands. He cares. And He will provide you with comfort. Jesus is characterized throughout Scripture as One who sympathizes with us. He is referred to as *"... a man of sorrows, and familiar with suffering ... surely He took up our infirmities and carried our sorrows."*[10]

Arena #2: Sob Over Your Sins

While we should lament our various losses, the primary emphasis of this beatitude is that you and I are to be sorrowful about our sinfulness. We would do well to echo Paul's agony when he summed up his struggle against sin by crying out, *"What a wretched man I am! Who will rescue me from this body of death?"*[11] Over 250 years ago, David Brainerd, a missionary to the American Indians, wrote this in his journal: *"In my morning devotions my soul was exceedingly melted, and I bitterly mourned over my exceeding sinfulness and vileness."*[12]

My guess is that most of us today don't use language like that to describe the state of our souls. But sorrow we must if we want to truly turn from our exceeding sinfulness. We must weep over what we have become, and we will when we recognize that our sin is not just unfortunate but reprehensible before a holy God. *"Grieve, mourn and wail. Change your laughter to mourning and your joy to gloom."*[13]

In his best-selling book, The Purpose Driven Life, Pastor Rick Warren suggests that we need to understand three words in this process.

Regret—This is when we remember things that we're sorry about: inappropriate conversations, causing pain to another, or being caught up in bad circumstances. I certainly have regret about some things I did growing up, (especially when my parents found out about it!).

Remorse—While regret is primarily in the mind, remorse comes from the heart. Instead of trying to make things right, a remorseful person often just stays in the pit of despondency. A person with remorse focuses on sin and its consequences; he or she may even love the sin but hate him or herself for engaging in the sin.

Repentance—When someone repents, they are serious about changing what they've been doing. The word literally means to change one's mind—to do an about-face and is often accompanied with tears.

When Peter recognized what he had done by denying Jesus three times, Matthew writes, *"he [Peter] wept bitterly."*[14] This is what Paul means when he tells us in 2 Corinthians: *"Godly sorrow brings repentance that leads to salvation and leaves no regret, but worldly sorrow brings death."*[15] As someone has said, "Sin will take you farther than you want to go, keep you longer than you want to stay, and cost you more than you want to pay."

In Luke 15, the prodigal son experienced godly sorrow. When he finally looked at what he was doing and how he was living, he *regretted* ever leaving home and hearth. Feelings of guilt and *remorse* overwhelmed him as he panhandled food from the pigs. When he recognized that he had sinned against both his heavenly Father and his earthly father, he *repented* and went home in search of forgiveness. He was met with love and grace from his dad even before he could make it up the driveway.

David committed adultery and murder. It wasn't until he saw his sins as an affront to the Almighty that he could be restored. He wrote, *"For I know my transgressions and my sin is always before me. Against You, You only, have I sinned and done what is evil in Your sight ..."*[16]

Jesus is really saying something like this: *Blessed is the one who mourns over his sin like one mourning for the dead.*

Are you sorry for your sins? Do you have deep sorrow about your sinfulness? There's a difference between the two. Until we understand, as Brainerd wrote, *"our exceeding sinfulness and vileness,"* we won't mourn like we should. And if we don't grieve over our guilt, we won't really understand grace and fully appreciate forgiveness.

Arena #3: Long For a Deep Compassion Regarding the Condition of Others

After reviewing our personal losses, looking within and coming face-to-face with our own sinfulness, Jesus also wants us to look around and cry about the state of those who don't yet know Him.

You may recall the scene immediately following Christ's triumphal entry into the city of Jerusalem. He was lauded, worshiped, and praised by the masses. At a point in His journey, Jesus sees the entire city of Jerusalem in a panoramic view. It was stunning in its beauty with gleaming white buildings and the lustrous gold of Herod's temple. But Jesus saw something different. Everyone was thrilled and happy with the exception of God's Son. *"As He approached Jerusalem and saw the city, He wept over it."*[17]

The word *wept* means to *burst into tears, to weep out loud, or to sob deeply.* This was more than just a tear streaming down His cheek. This same word is used in Mark 5:38 to describe how family members were crying over the death of a young daughter when the Bible says they were *"crying and wailing loudly."* He was not weeping because He was going to suffer and die. He was wailing loudly for the lost. His heart cry was for the people He saw all around Him. *"If you, even you, had only known on this day what would bring you peace—but now it is hidden from your eyes."*[18] And He wept.

The Scottish reformer, John Knox, constantly carried the burden of the Scottish people who were without Christ in his heart. Night after night, he prayed on the wooden floor of his house. When his wife pleaded with him to get some sleep, he answered, *"How can I sleep when my land is not saved?"*[19] He also would say repeatedly, *"Give me Scotland or I die!"*

We previously reviewed one of David Brainerd's journal entries. Here's another that gives us rich insight into a true missionary heart:

> *"I set apart this day for fasting and prayer to prepare me for ministry. In the forenoon, I felt a power of intercession for immortal souls. In the afternoon, God enabled me so to agonize in prayer that I was quite wet with sweat, though in the shade and cool wind. My soul was drawn out very much for the world: I gasped for multitudes of souls. I think I had more enlargement for sinners than for the children of God, though I felt as if I could spend my life in cries for both."*[20]

What about you? Do the things that break the heart of Jesus break your heart? When's the last time you wept for those who are lost and without Christ?

Arena #4: Wail and Weep Over Our World

There's one last arena in which we should grieve. As we look at our culture and the world at large, we have ample reason to be in agony. On December 26, 2004, a monster tsunami hit several countries in southern Asia and Africa, extinguishing the lives of more than 150,000 persons in one day. That's fifty "September 11ths." Read that last sentence again: don't miss its impact. We'll never forget the horror we felt when we saw nearly 3,000 people die on September 11, 2001, in New York, Washington, D.C., and Pennsylvania. As vocalist Alan Jackson asks in song, *"Where were you when the world stopped turning that September day?"*[21] The tsunami equaled 50 September 11ths! How do you begin to grasp a death toll like that? Believe it or not, it's a sobering reminder of an even greater tragedy.

Every day in our world 150,000 men, women, and children are swept into eternity. Every 24 hours we lose as many of our fellow human beings as were lost on the day of the December tsunami. The daily tsunami of death happens quietly and invisibly for most of us.

Eternity begins every day for 150,000 people in our world—many, if not most of them, are fully unprepared to meet God.

Tragically, many of the people who died in the surging waters of the tsunami did not have to perish. Had there been an adequate warning system in place, countless numbers might have been spared. Where and when people did receive a warning, they headed for high ground and survived. God has established a worldwide warning system to help people escape the tsunami of His judgment—to help them spend eternity with Him. That warning system is His people—people like us—you and me.

Jesus said to His followers, *"You will be My witnesses ..."*[22] That hasn't changed. He's counting on us to represent Him and sound the clarion call of warning to a dying world. The warning tells us that *"the wages of sin is death"*[23] and that only Jesus could (only Jesus did) die so we don't have to. Sin's death penalty can't be paid by doing good works and hoping at the end of life we've done enough to get us into heaven.

Someone had to die. Someone had to pay the penalty for the sin of mankind. Someone did—the Son of God. This isn't about Christianity being the only true religion. It's about Jesus being the only Savior there is because no one else even claimed to have died for our sin. If there was any other way to God, Jesus would not have suffered the horrible death that He did on the cross of Calvary.

When you consider that 150,000 people enter eternity every day and that they have no hope without Jesus, shouldn't that make us look at what we're spending our time on, what we're spending our money on, what we're spending our lives on? How can the warning system be silent when the tsunami is coming for more people every day? The responsibility rests squarely on the shoulders of those who belong to Jesus. *"We are therefore Christ's ambassadors, as though God were making His appeal through us. We implore you, on Christ's behalf: Be reconciled to God."*[24]

We've had a wakeup call watching so many swept into eternity at one time; reminding us that for 150,000 people every day, it's either heaven or hell. Think about your life in light of that reality. How can we be content to live lives that revolve only around ourselves and our little world? How can we be content for our local churches to be caught up in keeping all their programs going and just surviving when so many people die every day without ever having a chance of hearing the Gospel of Christ?

Don't we need to broaden the scope of our sometimes myopic prayers and pray as Jesus did: *"... that the world may know"*?[25] God so loved the world. How can we do less?

There is nothing more important than investing your life in getting the life-saving news about Jesus to as many people as possible while there's still time. You are God's warning system. To know the wave is coming and remain silent is to let people die who otherwise might have lived.

You may be thinking that the world in which we live can be very religious. The world was religious in Paul's day too; but it is just like today, not knowing the true righteousness of God. Paul writes to the church at Rome and says, *"Since they did not know the righteousness that comes from God and sought to establish their own, they did not submit to God's righteousness."*[26]

The book, "Gaily The Troubadour," by Arthur Guiterman, contains the following poem. Reading his observations, you wouldn't guess it was written nearly 70 years ago.

First dentistry was painless,
Then bicycles were chainless,
And carriages were horseless,
And many laws, enforceless.
Next, cookery was fireless,
Telegraphy was wireless,
Cigars were nicotineless
And coffee, caffeinless.
Soon oranges were seedless,

The putting green was weedless,
The college boy hatless,
The proper diet, fatless.
Now motor roads are dustless,
The latest steel is rustless,
Our tennis courts are sodless,
Our new religions, godless.[27]

We don't need more religion. The Bible is a book about relationship—not religion. Religion is man's attempt to reach God; a personal relationship with Jesus Christ is God's way of reaching down to man.

Let's do an exercise. Look at your watch and count out ten seconds. Did you do it? Good. Let me share with you some sobering facts. In those previous ten seconds, missiologists tells us that twenty-six people have just died on our planet. Of that twenty-six ...

Three were Buddhists;

Four were Hindus;

Five were Muslims;

Seven were Christians (and I use that term very loosely),

and seven were agnostics or atheists.

How many of them will spend eternity with Christ in Heaven? How many of them have slipped into a Christ-less eternity—Hell—in those ten seconds? How many went to be with the Lord? Three? Two? One? We don't really know, because we don't have access to the Lamb's Book of Life—the only Book that counts in this matter.

Let's say that all seven Christians were, in fact, born-again believers and devoted followers of Jesus Christ (that's a bit far-fetched because I have lumped together under the name "Christian," Protestant, Catholic, Greek Orthodox, Egyptian Coptic, etc., et al., and everything in-between.)

Even if all seven went to be with the Lord, we still discover that nineteen of twenty-six people have passed into a Christ-less eternity—and it happens every ten seconds. If we were to be honest with ourselves, the numbers are probably closer to twenty-four, twenty-five, or even twenty-six.

As Romans 10 teaches us, people the world over are very religious—but very few possess righteousness. The righteousness that God the Father demands is the righteousness that only comes from the Lord Jesus Christ; and only the Lord Jesus Christ can impart His righteousness to you and me.

Larry Libby, author and senior editor at Multnomah Publishing, writes of his own time of mourning and grieving:

Just yesterday, I went back to the hospital. I knew I shouldn't, but I did. Parking my car, I retraced my steps down the sidewalks as far as the south entrance.

My wife, Laura, and I went in through those doors a year ago this week. And those were the doors I walked out of to go home a few days later. Without her. My wife of 25 years went through her own door home, succumbing to cancer.

On yesterday's return journey, I stopped to pick one of the tiny lavender wildflowers growing along the hospital's rustic fitness trail. Last year, I picked a whole fistful, took them to her room, and presented my makeshift bouquet to her in a Styrofoam cup half-filled with water. For a moment, she smiled. A year later, the little flowers are blooming again, and new leaves are budding on the aspens. I made my way over to the same picnic bench where I sat and wept last year. And I wept again. Jesus said, 'Blessed are those who mourn, for they will be comforted.' Yet where is the blessedness of mourning? Where is the comfort? What I hear in Jesus' words these days is something like this: 'If you are filled with grief today, don't give into black despair. Cling to My promise: It will be better. The worst is here now, having its day. But the better is coming. Comfort is coming. I tell you, it is almost here.'

As temporary residents of a fallen world, we mourn for many reasons. We grieve over missed opportunities, broken dreams, unfulfilled desires, personal failures, dashed expectations, and difficult circumstances. We weep over lost health, lost innocence, and lost security. Disappointment and sorrow are as much a part of our planet's atmosphere as nitrogen and oxygen.

But Jesus, who is in a position to know, says it won't always be so. He says comfort is coming. I can hold on to that assurance.[28]

As we have discovered, there are different facets of mourning. No matter what level you may find yourself today, comfort is coming, brothers and sisters. Right now we mourn. As we do, however, we rest assured that comfort is coming from the loving hand of our Heavenly Father.

There is no life as empty as the self-centered life. There is no life as centered as the self-empty life.

—*John Maxwell*

Jesus calls us to His rest, and meekness is His method. The meek man cares not at all who is greater than he, for he has long ago decided that the esteem of the world is not worth the effort. The rest Christ offers is the rest of meekness, the blessed relief that comes when we accept ourselves for what we are and cease to pretend.

—*A. W. Tozer*

❖

CHAPTER FOUR

The Attitude of Humility

"Blessed are the meek, for they shall inherit the earth."
Matthew 5:5

I've recently read a book called *Franklin and Winston*. It examines the deep friendship forged between Winston Churchill and Franklin Roosevelt during World War Two. Churchill was quite a character in many respects; one thing he was particularly known for was his sharp sense of humor. He was once asked, "Doesn't it thrill you to know that every time you make a speech, the hall is packed to overflowing?"

"It's quite flattering," replied Sir Winston. "But whenever I feel that way, I always remember that if, instead of making a political speech I was being hanged, the crowd would be twice as big."[1]

That type of thinking, while self-deprecatory, rightly leads to an understanding of one's self. It is, in a sense, a right attitude of humility; Churchill's quote is a type of biblical meekness.

Defining Meekness

This beatitude is difficult for us to grasp because some of us equate meekness with weakness. In fact, if you were to go and tell someone, "I think you are a meek person" I'm not sure it would be received as a compliment. My thesaurus lists some synonyms to meekness that aren't very flattering:

acquiescent, compliant, deferential, docile, lenient, lowly,
manageable, milquetoast, modest, nothing, pabulum,

passive, schnook, soft, spineless, spiritless, subdued, submissive, tame, timid, tolerant, unassuming, unpretentious, unresisting, weak, weak-kneed, wishy-washy, yielding, zero.

It's no wonder we don't want to be called meek, if that's what the word means! But since this characteristic is part of the definition of a disciple, we need to understand what Jesus meant when He said it.

The word *meek* was used in contradictory contexts that, taken together, will help us understand how we can demonstrate meekness in our lives.

Meekness is a Happy Medium

In the Greek culture of the first century, one heavily influenced by Aristotelian teaching and philosophy, virtue was described as the attitude between two extremes.

On one hand, we have the person who cannot keep a dollar in his or her pocket—they are spenders. On the other hand, there is the miser. The miser can squeeze the life out of every penny. (That reminds me: have you heard the joke about the miserly Swedish widow? It seems her husband passed away, and she called the local newspaper to have his obituary placed therein. The editor asked her, "What would you like it to say?" She replied, "Sven Johanssen died." Incredulously, the newspaper-man responded, "That's it?" She said, "That's it." He replied, "But for the same price you get six words." She said, "Okay, add: Volvo for sale.")

In between these two extremes—spenders and misers—lies the virtue of generosity. The Greek mind defined meekness as being balanced between *too much anger and too little anger.* The meek person was neither timid nor given to fits of rage. In other words, you are meek when you are always angry at the right time and never angry at the wrong time.

Greek physicians used the word *meek* to describe a soothing medicine. If too little medicine is given, it won't work properly;

if too much is prescribed, it can hurt instead of heal. The proper amount of medication can work wonders.

Meek was also used to describe a gentle breeze that blew in from the ocean. Wind can rage and do great damage; but when it blows gently, it brings soothing comfort.

These are all happy mediums. Too much can be harmful; so can too little; but a happy medium is just right.

Meekness is Accepting the Authority I Am Under

Meekness was commonly used to describe an animal that had been domesticated. The word picture here is of a wild stallion that had been tamed. A broken horse is still very powerful, but its power is now under the control of the bridle. The steed answers to a command; he responds to his reigns. In other words, you are meek when every instinct, every impulse, every passion is under control. You are blessed when you are entirely self-controlled.

Ah, but now we are faced with a dilemma! We cannot control our impulses, urges, or passions when and how we want. If we could, we wouldn't be in the trouble we are now in! We cannot be fully self-controlled. Complete self-control is beyond our capacity as human beings.

Psychologist Walter Mischel once conducted an experiment at a preschool on the Stanford University campus. Children were told that they could have a single treat, such as a marshmallow, "right now." If they would wait, however, while the experimenter ran an errand, each child could have two marshmallows. The adult left the room full of preschoolers, who were being observed through one-way glass. Some preschoolers ate the single marshmallow immediately, but others were able to wait—for what to them must have seemed an eternity of twenty minutes. To sustain themselves in their struggle, they covered their eyes so they wouldn't see the fluffy temptation. Some rested their heads on their arms and talked to themselves. A few children sang; some even tried to sleep. The plucky youngsters who held out received the two-marshmallow reward.

The interesting part of this experiment came in the follow-up. The children who, as four-year olds, had been able to wait for the two marshmallows were, as adolescents, still able to delay gratification in pursuing their goals. They were more socially competent and self-assertive and better able to cope with life's frustrations. In contrast, the kids who grabbed the one marshmallow were, as adolescents, more likely to be stubborn, indecisive, and stressed.[2]

If only life were a choice between one or two marshmallows! Try as we might, we simply cannot control our every impulse and urge.

Having acquired the background knowledge on the words *meek* and *meekness*, we now need to fully understand what meekness means as Jesus is using the word in the fifth chapter of Matthew.

Meekness is Pride-Banishing Humility

Jesus is speaking of the blessing for the person who is completely under God's control. He wants us to grasp the fact that only in serving Him and living under His influence do we really find blessing, joy, and peace.

The common thread in how we have so far described meekness is that it represents different forms of power that can be used for positive purposes or for evil intentions. The commentator William Barclay refers to the meek man as one *"... who has every instinct under control. Every impulse, every passion, every ounce of strength has been harnessed."*[3]

The Greeks always contrasted the word Jesus is using here—*praotēs*—with another word—*hupsēlokardia*—being lofty of heart. The happy medium to which Jesus is referring is humility before God that banishes all human pride.

Humility is one virtue—one attitude—which is so difficult to grasp! Who among us does not struggle with pride?

One of the last century's great preachers was Dr. Harry Ironside. If you've ever taught the Bible, you've probably read some of his commentaries. Dr. Ironside was once inwardly convicted about his lack of humility. A friend recommended, as a remedy, that he march through the streets of downtown Chicago wearing a sandwich board, shouting the humility-themed Scripture verses painted on the board for all to hear. Dr. Ironside agreed to this venture. When he returned to his study and removed the board, he said to his colleague, "I'll bet there's not another man in town that would do that!" [4]

Jesus is teaching us that we are to possess a humility by which we understand and accept our limitations, our ignorance, and our weaknesses.

With this fuller background, let's take a look at what this meekness and humility looks like in the life of a God-follower.

Illustrating Meekness

Did you know that only two people in the Bible were ever called meek? Jesus describes Himself that way in Matthew 11:29. He said, *"Take my yoke upon you, and learn of me; for I am meek and lowly in heart ..."* [5] The other example is found in the Old Testament. Numbers 12:3 identifies Moses as being *"... very meek, above all the men which were upon the face of the earth."* [6]

I don't know about you, but I wouldn't automatically put Moses in the "meek man" category. Several years prior to the Numbers account, he became incensed with rage and murdered an Egyptian. He stood up to Pharaoh, led the Israelites across the Red Sea, and climbed Mount Sinai where he met with the Lord Almighty.

Numbers 12 tells us that Moses had married a Cushite woman and was, therefore, openly criticized by Aaron and

Miriam for doing so. They actually challenged Moses' leadership qualifications by saying, *"Has the Lord spoken only through Moses? Hasn't He also spoken through us?"[7]* What's really frightening is the sentence at the end of verse two: *"And the Lord heard this."[8]* The narrative continues: *"And suddenly the Lord said to Moses and Aaron and to Miriam, 'You three come out to the tent of meeting.' So the three of them came out."[9]* God then vindicated Moses and turned Miriam white with leprosy.

Now, with all that going on, what was Moses doing? Nothing. His first recorded words in this story are in verse 13 when he cries out for God to heal Miriam. Moses didn't fight back; he didn't seek revenge; he didn't argue. Instead, he kept quiet and let the Lord take up his cause. When Moses did finally open his mouth, it was to intercede for the one who had challenged and chastised him. What does this Old Testament story teach us about meekness? A meek person refrains from revenge and leaves vindication with God.

Secondly, there's a very helpful book penned by John Ortberg titled, *Everybody's Normal Till You Get to Know Them.*[10] He humorously makes the point that we're all weird and pretend to be healthier and holier than we really are. He says that we're a lot like the porcupine, with over 30,000 quills attached to its body. Each quill can be driven deeply into an enemy. As a general rule, porcupines have two methods for handling relationships: *withdrawal* and *attack.* They either head for the hills or lock and load. Ortberg says that each of us carry our own little arsenal of quills. Our barbs have names like rejection, condemnation, judgment, resentment, arrogance, selfishness, envy, and contempt. A meek person will not only avoid flinging quills at others, but when barbs come his way, he will absorb them without lashing back.

Another Old Testament example illustrates this well. Abraham exhibited meekness when he gave his nephew, Lot, the option to choose the best of two options. Abraham had received the promise of a blessing from God. He was older than Lot, and the leader of their expedition; but he didn't want the quills to fly. The Bible says, "So Abram said to Lot, 'Let's not have any quarreling between you and me, or between your herdsmen and mine, for we are brothers.'"[11] Abraham trusted God instead of justifiably laying into Lot. We learn from Abraham's actions that a meek person lives with a Spirit-controlled desire to put the interests of another ahead of his or her own.

A final Old Testament example: David exhibited meekness when he could have slaughtered King Saul and claimed the kingdom for himself. David's political and military power was on the rise; he was being encouraged by his cohorts to slay Saul. He kept his ambitions bridled when he said in 1 Samuel 24:6, *"The LORD forbid that I should do such a thing to my master, the LORD's anointed, or lift my hand against him; for he is the anointed of the LORD."*[12] Since David delighted in the Lord and trusted His timing, he could wait patiently for God to work everything out. I find it very interesting that David never bragged in the Psalms about killing Goliath. He was meek and humble because He trusted God. David certainly modeled meekness. Therefore, a meek person recognizes that God is in control.

We've defined and illustrated meekness. We now have a good understanding of how meekness is defined and how it can appear in a believer's life. Jesus finishes His sentence in Matthew 5 by saying, *"... they shall inherit the earth ..."*[13] What does that mean?

Inheriting the Earth

It's no accident that meekness follows being poor in spirit and being blessed when we mourn. It's at this point that we realize we have no real power of our own and that the power God does give us, must be harnessed for His holy purposes. Meekness is not a sign of weakness but of great inner strength.

This beatitude contains a surprising promise. The meek shall *"inherit the earth."* It's those that have their spirits bridled by Christ who will inherit the land.

This is unexpected. We would think that the strong and mighty inherit the land. Meek people get nowhere; they are trampled underfoot; others ride roughshod over them! It is only the tough, the overbearing who make it to the top. Now hear this! The condition upon which we enter our spiritual inheritance in Christ is not by might but by meekness.

The godless may throw their power around; but in actual fact, they are powerless. They possess nothing; they are grasping at straws. The meek, on the other hand, although they may be temporally despised, disenfranchised, and looked down upon by their fellow man, know what it is to live under the rule and reign of Jesus Christ. Then one day, there will be a new heaven and a new earth for them to inherit. If you are a man or woman who is truly meek, you may well be described as having nothing but possessing everything!

I recall reading of a man who was sitting on a curb crying. When he was asked what was wrong, he said, "I just found out that Rockefeller, the richest man in the world, has died." The person then asked, "Why are you crying? You're not a relative of his, are you?" To which the man replied, "No! That's why I'm crying!"

If you know Christ, you are an heir of everything that is His. You'll receive some of it now and more of it later. There will be an inheritance for the meek in the sweet by-and-by and in the nasty day-to-day. The word *inherit* means to possess. Right now it seems like the wicked reign, and the meek take a back seat; but Jesus said that one day, the meek will come marching in. Believers who live out this beatitude have nothing, yet possess everything.

A Meekness Makeover

Maybe you have viewed the TV show, *Extreme Makeover.* People are physically transformed through exercise, diet, and surgery. God wants to give each of us a meekness makeover. How may we receive one?

Abandon Yourself to Christ.

Though Jesus gave Himself a number of figurative titles such as the *Good Shepherd* and the *Light of the World,* when it comes to actually describing His character with specific virtues, there are very few self-portraits. Here's how Jesus describes Himself in Matthew 11:28-30: *"Come to me, all you who are weary and burdened, and I will give you rest. Take my yoke upon you and learn from me, for I am gentle and humble in heart, and you will find rest for your souls. For my yoke is easy and my burden is light."*[14] In the King James Version, we read, *"For I am meek and lowly in heart ..."*

We must first come to Christ and roll our burdens on Him. Then we yield to Him by taking His yoke upon us. When an ox accepts the yoke, it models meekness. It is still very powerful, but its power is under the control of another. Jesus is saying, "I want you to be connected to Me so that we can walk side-by-side. We will work together and walk through the trials of life as one. As you yield to My yoke, you will learn from Me and discover that I am meek; and you will gradually become more gentle yourself. You will also discover that what I offer you is a perfect fit for who you are. My teachings are not heavy but easy, and my burden is light. Give Me your burdens, and I will give you rest."

Jesus invites us to learn from Him. A.W. Tozer wrote, *"Jesus calls us to His rest, and meekness is His method. The meek man cares not at all who is greater than he, for he has long ago decided that the esteem of the world is not worth the effort. The rest Christ offers is the rest of meekness, the blessed relief that comes when we accept ourselves for what we are and cease to pretend."*[15]

Accept the Word of God.

If you want to be meek, then it's essential that you cultivate a submission to God's Word. In fact, the Bible is the bit and bridle that controls our wild spirits. James 1:21 challenges us to receive God's revelation with an openness to let it change us: *"Therefore lay aside all filthiness and overflow of wickedness, and receive with meekness the implanted word, which is able to save your souls."*[16]

Note the word *receive* above. There are two Greek words translated *receive*. One has the idea of grasping and reaching out. It's what some of us do with the Bible as we study the facts and put them in our heads. The other word means to *invite with humility* and has the idea not of taking but of receiving. Have you ever welcomed and received the Word into your heart and life regardless of what it says? If you want to grow in meekness, you must yield to Scripture.

Attach Yourself to the Spirit of God.

If we want to be meek, we must first learn from the Master who is meek, we must welcome the Word, and we must attach ourselves to the Spirit of God. How is that accomplished? Submission. Paul mentions meekness as a fruit of the Spirit, which can only come from the Holy Spirit.[17] Fruit is not something we do; it's what we display. Our responsibility is clear from Scripture: *"Since we live by the Spirit, let us keep in step with the Spirit."*[18] The key is not to work harder but to worship more fully; not to try more but to trust more.

When was the last time you prayed to be filled with the Holy Spirit? Have you ever asked Him to make you meeker? Meekness comes about when we surrender to the Holy Spirit and meekness manifests in us by a gentle spirit within that is founded upon an unshakable confidence in God. Someone has well said, *"Meekness is not merely the absence of pride and arrogance, so much as it is the fullness of the presence of God, where pride and arrogance cannot abide."*

Associate With the People of God.

While it's certainly true that it's easier to get close to someone when they have no quills, the truth of the matter is that we all have the capacity to attack and wound one another. In Scripture, meekness is frequently contrasted with words like harsh, violent, unrelenting, strict, and severe. A meek person seeks to give grace to others and puts up with imperfect people. Ephesians 4:2 says, *"Be completely humble and gentle; be patient, bearing with one another in love."*[19]

We need to be reminded that no one is perfect, except God alone. Your spouse will disappoint you. Your kids will fail you. Your friends will let you down. Your church will drop the ball at times. Your pastor won't meet all your expectations. The time will come when you will have a legitimate gripe. You will be right, and they will be wrong. Here is the crossroad of meekness. Which path will you take? Will you launch some quills of condemnation, or give them the cold shoulder? Or will you grant grace and gentleness?

Before you make that decision, remind yourself how gentle Jesus is toward imperfect people just like you. We can choose to live our lives disappointed and angry with everyone around us, or we can be armed with the virtue of meekness and enter into the blessing of authentic community. *"Be completely humble and gentle [this is the word "meek"]; be patient, bearing with one another in love. Make every effort to keep the unity of the Spirit through the bond of peace."*[20]

Address Yourself to God's Mission

When people today see believers living lives of meekness, they will wonder what's happening! Some of us are pretty harsh with those who don't know Jesus. That's one reason Peter challenges us to be ready to let people know why we have such foundational hope; we're to let them know about Christ and all He has done with *"gentleness (meekness) and respect."*[21]

Everything is ours, if we are in Christ.

Many years ago, Christian professor Stuart Blackie of the University of Edinburgh was listening to his students as they presented oral readings. When one young man rose to begin his recitation, he held his book in his left hand. According to the professor's strict classroom rules for public readings, this was the wrong hand. The professor thundered, "Take your book in your right hand, and be seated!" At this harsh rebuke, the student held up his right arm. He didn't have a right hand! The other students shifted uneasily in their chairs.

For a moment Professor Blackie hesitated. Then he made his way to the student, put his arm around him and with tears streaming from his eyes said, "I never knew about it. Please, will you forgive me?" His humble apology made a lasting impact on that young man.

That story was being related some years later at a large gathering of believers. At the close of the meeting a man came forward, turned to the crowd and raised his right arm. It ended at the wrist. He said, "I was that student. Professor Blackie led me to Christ, but he never could have done it if he had not made the wrong right."

Meekness. Do you desire this character quality in your life? Then consciously choose to commit all of your life and will to Christ's care and control. Keep short accounts with God and stay willing to right wrongs—never considering your own embarrassment, but only cherishing the virtue of humility you bestow on others.

I have been reading the Beatitudes and can claim at least one of the blessings therein unfolded. It is the blessing pronounced upon those who hunger and thirst after righteousness.

—*Abraham Lincoln in a letter to a friend*

❖

CHAPTER FIVE

The Attitude of Satisfaction

"Blessed are those who hunger and thirst for righteousness,
for they will be filled."
Matthew 5:6

There is a hamburger served at Denny's Beer Barrel Pub, 1423 Dorey Street in Clearfield, Pennsylvania. It's called Ye Olde 96er. The sandwich has six pounds of hamburger meat with another five pounds of fixins'. That's a lot of sandwich —a total of eleven pounds!

The Pub offers a prize to anyone who can eat it in three hours. Many have tried, but no one has accomplished the feat in less than the required three hours. Not until January, 2005. The prize winner was Kate Stelnick, a 100-pound, 18-year-old college freshman from Princeton, New Jersey. She devoured the sandwich in two-hours and fifty-four minutes.

What is in the beefy gastronomic monstrosity, besides six pounds of hamburger? Hold on to your stomach! Two whole tomatoes, a half-head of lettuce, twelve slices of American cheese, a full cup of peppers, two entire onions, and a river of mayonnaise, ketchup, and mustard. The cost? A mere $23.95.

If your head is not spinning yet or your tummy doing flip-flops, let me ask you: "Do you think you could consume that burger?" Katie did. Without a strategy, Stelnick first went at the tomatoes then dug in to the burger, drinking lots of water between bites. "Once the burger got cold, it was a little gross," she said. "The last 20 minutes were the hardest, and I credit my friends for cheering me on to the finish." "She looked a little flush there at the end," said the pub owner.

Since she finished the burger six minutes under the three-hour time limit, Kate received the $23.95 burger free-of-charge and a $75 gift certificate toward Denny's Beer Barrel Pub merchandise. To top it off, she will have her name engraved on a plaque.

If you're wondering how Stelnick felt the day after her burger bash, physically she didn't feel any different. "I didn't get sick, but I'm not going to be eating hamburgers for a while," she laughed. "The only problem is when I told my parents what I did, they were pretty upset—not because I ate the burger, but because I drove five hours to do it." [1]

It's amazing what some people will do with food, isn't it? In this beatitude, Jesus is calling us to hunger and thirst for something—it's not an eleven-pound burger—it is righteousness. Let's explore His words.

The Requirement to Meet

The word Jesus uses for *hunger* refers to the desperate craving that a starving person has for food. He is so famished that he becomes desperate for any food. The word *thirst* means to painfully feel the need for water. This is more than just needing a sip; it means to be parched and dehydrated to the point of pain.

Everywhere else in the Bible, hunger is described as being satisfied by just having a couple of bites that will last until the next regular meal. Thirst is similarly described: just allow me a sip of water until I can really quench my thirst later with a fresh, cold drink. Only here in Matthew 5 are these words used in this sense: To hunger and thirst means to be dissatisfied with our present situation.

In essence, in order for our lives to change so that we can experience the spiritual satisfaction that only the Savior can provide, we must first admit that we are starving and thirsting.

We all need change at some level in our lives so that we can come to this point. This reminds me of the man who pleaded with his psychiatrist for help: "Doc, you've got to help me! I can't stop believing that I'm a dog." The psychiatrist responded with a question: "How long have you had this problem?" To which the man replied, "Ever since I was a puppy."

Hopefully, any problems you have are different from that one; but my guess is that the teachings of Jesus in the "Beatitudes" shake all of us up to some extent. We know we're not who we're supposed to be, and we realize that there's more to life than this world can offer.

Do you want to change? If so, then it's time to develop an appetite for the Almighty. To gain that ...

Watch What You Eat!

Some of us have been consuming things that will not satisfy because they were never designed by the Creator to bring us fulfillment. One reason you may not be hungering for holiness is because frankly, you feel pretty full. Proverbs teaches us, *"He who is full loathes honey, but to the hungry even what is bitter tastes sweet."*[2] Maybe it's time to admit that you are a spiritual junk food addict.

What have you been eating spiritually? Let me explain. Perhaps you're ingesting things that feel good at first, but later on they leave you disillusioned and depressed. Or maybe you feel pretty full today, but it may not last because you're just feeding your appetite with things that will never fully satisfy. The sooner you realize that your longings can only be filled by the Lover of your soul, the sooner you will be motivated to change.

Jesus is teaching us that until we come to the place where we have single-mindedness in our passion for God, we will never experience true satisfaction. The question then becomes: Do you have a passion for God? Do you *hunger* and *thirst* after righteousness? Is this your desire? Is this what you want above all else? Are you starving for God? You will find nothing else which will satisfy that hunger.

Days before his death, Abraham Lincoln confided to a friend that he had been yearning for a sweeter, more satisfying faith. "I have been reading the Beatitudes," he writes, "and can at least claim the blessing that is pronounced upon those who hunger and thirst after righteousness."[3] He sought and found only that which God supplied.

Isaiah relates God's astonishment that we fill our lives with things that were never designed to be fulfilling: *"Why waste your money on what really isn't food? Why work hard for something that doesn't satisfy? Listen carefully to Me, and you will enjoy the very best foods. Pay close attention! Come to Me and live. I will promise you the eternal love and loyalty that I promised David."*[4]

Only God satisfies. We must, therefore, come to the place where we are hungry and thirsty only for God and God alone. We must desire Him so passionately that our desire causes us to do something about it. Nothing less than this sort of passion will cause us to live properly. When the prodigal son was hungry, he turned to the husks that he was feeding the pigs. When he was starving, he turned to his father.[5]

Are you munching on material things in the hope that they will fill you? Are you snacking on a sexual sin for satisfaction? Are you consuming your career as if success will meet your needs? Do you salivate over sports more than you should? Are you drinking to dull the despair you are feeling? Then willfully choose to turn from these cravings and turn to God; His Word will cause you to crave Him every day.

The Term "Hunger and Thirst" Means to Desire Whole and Total Righteousness

Jesus Christ understood this. When He was tested and tempted three times by Satan in the wilderness, He quoted Scripture every time. The Word of God has the power to defeat

Satan and his designs in our lives. Jesus chose righteousness and the things of God over and above anything and everything Satan could throw at Him.

Jesus also taught this principle to the woman He encountered at the well in the fourth chapter of John. She had been married five times and was now living with a man who wasn't her husband. Jesus said, *"Everyone who drinks this water will be thirsty again, but whoever drinks the water I give him will never thirst. Indeed, the water I give him will become in him a spring of water welling up to eternal life."*[6]

What will you feed your spirit? Worldly principles? Desires? Possessions? Or the truth of Jesus which will last a lifetime, not leaving you hungry again in an hour? Immediately after His encounter with the woman at the well, we find Jesus addressing His disciples. *"He said to them, 'I have food to eat that you do not know about.' The disciples therefore were saying to one another, 'No one brought Him anything to eat, did he?' Jesus said to them, 'My food is to do the will of Him who sent Me, and to accomplish His work.'"*[7]

This isn't just a principle confined to the Gospel accounts. The apostle Paul understood and taught this as well. He wrote to the Christians at Philippi: *"Yes, everything else is worthless when compared with the priceless gain of knowing Christ Jesus my Lord. I have discarded everything else, counting it all as garbage, so that I may have Christ."*[8]

Paul is speaking of having a healthy spiritual appetite. Our doctors always tell us that an appetite is a sign of health. Do you recall the last time you were sick? Accompanying your ailment was a lack of appetite. As a pastor, I often talk with persons who are struggling with illness. I know they're on the mend when I hear them tell me, "I'm feeling better; I'm starting to get my appetite back."

My wife, Darlene, has a little sign hanging in our home. It reads, "Is Chocolate a Fruit or Vegetable?" Our world is full of "chocoholics"! Here are some of their rules:

- *If you've got melted chocolate all over your hands, you're eating it too slowly.*

- *Chocolate covered raisins, cherries, orange slices, and strawberries all count as fruit, so eat as many as you want.*

- *If calories are an issue, store your chocolate on top of the fridge. Calories are afraid of heights, and they will jump out of the chocolate to protect themselves.*

- *Diet tip: Eat a chocolate bar before each meal. It'll take the edge off your appetite, and you'll eat less.*

It's time to eat what is good so that your soul may live. Gorge yourself on God, and turn away from food and drink that will never satisfy. The hunger and thirst of your life that cannot be satisfied by anything in this world is the constant reminder of God to remember that we were made for another world—we were made for Him.

If we want to grow spiritually, we must crave the righteousness, the presence, of God Himself. The psalmist understood this concept well. Look at just a few of the heart-cries of David:

As the deer pants for the water brooks, so my soul pants for Thee, O God.[9]

A psalm of David. When he was in the Desert of Judah. O God, You are my God, earnestly I seek You; my soul thirsts for You, my body longs for You, in a dry and weary land where there is no water. I have seen You in the sanctuary and beheld Your power and your glory. Because Your love is better than life, my lips will glorify You. I will praise You as long as I live, and in Your name I will lift up my hands. My soul will be satisfied as with the richest of foods; with singing

lips my mouth will praise You. On my bed I remember You;
I think of You through the watches of the night. Because You
are my help, I sing in the shadow of Your wings. My soul
clings to You; Your right hand upholds me.[10]

The Reason to Hunger and Thirst

Jesus says there's something for which we are to hunger: righteousness. Righteousness is a word that conjures up many images. What exactly does it mean? The theologian John Stott tells us that legal righteousness is justification, or being in a right relationship with God. Paul tells us that the Jews pursued righteousness but failed to attain it because they pursued it in the wrong manner.[11] They sought to establish their own righteousness and did not submit to God's righteousness which is found only in the person of the Lord Jesus Christ Himself.

Righteousness not only contains a legal element; it also contains a moral element. This is a righteousness of character and conduct which pleases God. False righteousness seeks to conform to external religious rules; God is looking for an inner righteousness of heart, mind, and motive.

Additionally, righteousness has a social element. Biblical righteousness is more than a right relationship with God on one hand and a moral righteousness of character and behavior on the other hand. It is more than a public and personal affair; it also includes social righteousness. This, as the prophets teach us, is seeking man's liberation from oppression, while promoting civil freedoms and liberty. The Founding Fathers of the United States called it "freedom of conscience."

I am a student of American history and am convinced the framers of the Constitution had this in mind when they wrote about the pursuit of liberty and that all men are created equal. This social righteousness carries over into the integrity with which you conduct your business and personal affairs; maintaining honor in your home and family affairs.

How important is this pursuit after righteousness? Pastor John MacArthur writes, "Righteousness is not an optional spiritual supplement but a spiritual necessity." [12]

There is a Reward to Gain!

Author Marion Gilbert relates the following humorous story: "One morning I opened the door to get the newspaper and was surprised to see a strange little dog with our paper in his mouth. Delighted with this unexpected 'delivery service,' I fed him some treats. The following morning I was horrified to see the same dog sitting in front of our door, wagging his tail, surrounded by eight newspapers. "I spent the rest of that morning returning the papers to my neighbors." [13]

Who knows what occurs in the mind of our canine companions, but our furry friend was somehow expecting an immediate reward for his efforts. The Lord Jesus calls us to look beyond our immediate satisfaction to what He is preparing for us in eternity. He has made wonderful provisions for our future with Him. The psalmist writes, "... for He satisfies the thirsty and fills the hungry with good things." [14]

Imagine for a moment with me that you are a dinner guest at a friend's home. You arrive and soon approach a magnificent buffet-table and espy a golden-brown turkey, fluffy mashed potatoes, lump-less gravy, buttery vegetables, and fresh home-baked pies. Your friends have awaited your arrival so the feast can begin. You say, "No thanks. I couldn't wait, so I ate a bologna sandwich and bag of pork rinds on the way."

Ridiculous? Who would choose a bologna sandwich over a turkey dinner with all the trimmings? Hungering and thirsting after righteousness brings a reward: *"for they will be filled."* Don't settle for a bag lunch when you can have the whole feast. It's worth the wait. The glories that await us in heaven far outweigh any trials or tribulations we might have to deal with here. [15]

How Should This Beatitude Affect Our Lives?

When I am spiritually hungry and thirsty I will pursue holiness more than happiness.

Holiness is a word that conjures up images in our minds. We think of holier-than-thou, self-proclaimed saints who do not live a "normal" life. We don't think holiness has much to do with us. Isn't it reserved for those who have received some special, mystical calling from God to an ascetic lifestyle? For an answer, let's turn to John Brown, a nineteenth-century Scottish theologian. He writes, "Holiness does not consist in mystic speculations, enthusiastic fervors, or uncommanded austerities; it consists in thinking as God thinks, and willing as God wills."[16]

The Bible says, *"Ascribe to the Lord the glory due His name. Bring an offering and come before Him; worship the Lord in the splendor of His holiness."*[17] As the priests would minister in beautiful priestly attire, Ezra called all Israel to *"worship the Lord in the beauty of holiness."* What constitutes the "beauty of holiness?" Beauty in a holy life can be manifested in a number ways. Let's consider a few.

The Beauty of a Holy Life

Paul prays for his fellow believers: *"... that you may walk worthy of the Lord, fully pleasing Him, being fruitful in every good work and increasing in the knowledge of God; strengthened with all might, according to His glorious power, for all patience and long suffering with joy."*[18] He is exhorting us to live a beautiful life that will be well-pleasing to our Lord.

The Beauty of Holy Speech

"Let your speech always be with grace, seasoned with salt, that you may know how you ought to answer each one."[19]

The psalmist stresses the importance of our speech when he wrote: *"Let the words of my mouth and the mediation of my heart be acceptable in Thy sight, O Lord, my strength [literally: Rock] and*

Redeemer.[20] A holiness regarding the words that come from our mouths is beautiful to God.

The Beauty of a Holy Disposition

We should pattern our ways after our Lord Jesus Christ. Consider what the Scripture says: *"Let this mind be in you which was also in Christ Jesus, who, being in the form of God, did not consider it robbery to be equal with God, but made Himself of no reputation, taking the form of a bond servant, and coming in the likeness of men. And being found in appearance as a man, He humbled Himself and became obedient to the point of death, even the death of the cross."*[21]

If we as Christians would only keep this exhortation before us, how different our lives and actions would be! The great nineteenth-century preacher, C. H. Spurgeon, had this passage in mind when he wrote,

> *Such men are among Satan's best allies. They pull down by their lives what ministers build with their lips. They cause the chariot wheels of the Gospel to drive heavily. They supply the children of this world with a never-ending excuse for remaining as they are.*

> *'I cannot see the use of so much religion,' said an irreligious tradesman not long ago; 'I observe that some of my customers are always talking about the Gospel, and faith, and election, and the blessed promises, and so forth; and yet these very people think nothing of cheating me of pence and half-pence when they have an opportunity. Now, if religious persons can do such things, I do not see what good there is in religion.' I grieve to be obliged to write such things, but I fear that Christ's name is too often blasphemed because of the lives of Christians. Let us take heed lest the blood of souls should be required at our hands. From murder of souls by inconsistency and loose walking, good Lord, deliver us!*

Oh, for the sake of others, if for no other reason, let us strive to be holy!

Holiness presses us to strive after the character and qualities of Jesus. Jesus was:

• Morally pure: *"For we do not have a High Priest who can not sympathize with our weaknesses, but was in all points tempted as we are, yet without sin."* [22]

• Gentle and humble: *"gentle and humble in heart."* [23]

• Compassionate: *"But when He saw the multitudes, He was moved with compassion for them, because they were weary and scattered, like sheep having no shepherd."* [24]

• Forgiving: *"When Jesus had raised Himself up and saw no one but the woman, He said to her, 'Woman, where are your accusers? Has no one condemned you?' She said, 'No one, Lord.' And Jesus said to her, 'Neither do I condemn you; go and sin no more.'"* [25]

Somehow we concocted a wrong-headed idea of holiness. C. S. Lewis wrote, *"How little people know who think that holiness is dull. When one meets the real thing, it is irresistible."* [26] Let us obey God's Word to us through His apostle Paul, when he commands, *"... let us cleanse ourselves from all filthiness of the flesh and spirit, perfecting holiness in the fear of God."* [27] When we are spiritually hungry and thirsty, we will agree with God that sin is sin.

Little Johnny's father caught him in telling a lie. Dad said, "Don't you know the difference between right and wrong?" Johnny affirmed that he did. His dad said, "But you always choose the wrong!" Johnny said, "I know, Dad. And here you thought it was all guesswork."

Johnny's dad said it was wrong; Johnny said it was guesswork; God says it is sin. Sometimes we just want to play around with the things that God hates; we want to see how close we can get to the line without crossing over.

The story is told of a king who was looking for a new chariot driver. He interviewed three drivers, and asked each of them how close they could come to the edge of a certain well-known cliff that had a 500-foot drop-off while at full gallop and not plunge over the edge.

The first driver said, "Sire, I can get within three cubits of the edge without going over."

The second said, "Sire, I can come as close as one cubit and still not fall over the edge."

The third said, "Sire, I am going to stay as far away from the edge of the cliff as I can."

The king chose the third man as his driver. We should not try to be close to the enticements of the world, but stay as far away as we can. In the Old Testament, Samson was an example of someone who played with fire and got burned. He had it all—good looks and great physical strength—while possessing little spiritual or moral strength. He married a girl who wasn't Jewish.

There's nothing wrong with that today; but in Samson's day, God had presented some very specific laws to His chosen people: Jews were not to marry non-Jews because of the latter's habit of worshiping false gods. Samson chose to disobey God's law and hitched himself—not only to a Gentile—but a Gentile prostitute. He gave in to the charms of Delilah, revealing to her a previously unknown secret: the source of his amazing strength.

The result of playing around with sin was that Samson's eyes were gouged out and he became a slave. He chose against holiness and was humiliated, suffering a tremendous loss of dignity and self-respect, and his poor choices ultimately resulted in his death. Scripture adds a sobering postscript to Samson's life: "... *he did not know that the Lord had left him.*"[28]

When I am spiritually hungry and thirsty, I will be obedient to God.

God calls us to obey Him in every area of life: in everything we say, and in everything we do. But be warned! If we're not careful we can allow our obedience to become a performance. Let's compare the two:

- Obedience is seeking God with your whole heart. Performance is having a quiet time because you'll feel guilty if you don't.

- Obedience is finding ways to let the Word of God dwell in you richly. Performance is quickly scanning a passage so you can check it off your Bible reading plan.

- Obedience is inviting guests to your home for dinner. Performance is feeling anxiety about whether every detail of the meal will be perfect.

- Obedience is following God's prompting to start a small group. Performance is reluctance to let anyone else lead the group because they might not do it as well as you.

- Obedience is saying yes to whatever God asks of you. Performance is saying yes to whatever people ask of you.

- Obedience is following the promptings of God's Spirit. Performance is following a list of man-made requirements.

- Obedience springs from your reverence of Almighty God. Performance springs from fear of failure.

Hungering and thirsting for righteousness will be fleshed out in our obedience.

When I am spiritually hungry and thirsty, I will not know spiritual indifference.

Singer and songwriter Keith Green described spiritual indifference this way:

"My eyes are dry, my faith is old, my heart is hard, my prayers are cold. And I know what I ought to be, alive to You and dead to me."[29]

We have probably all experienced this in our own lives. This is not what we should desire or need. What we need is a heart which is hungry for God. What we need is a passion restored. Green goes on to say in this same song,

"Oh, what can be done with an old heart like mine?
Soften it, Lord, with oil and wine.
The oil is You, Your Spirit of love.
Come wash me anew in the wine of Your blood."[30]

If you want to truly be satisfied, you must desire God. We must desire Him with all that is within us. The Old Testament law said, *"And you shall love the LORD your God with all your heart and with all your soul and with all your might."*[31] An Old Testament prophet reminded, *"And you will seek Me and find Me, when you search for Me with all your heart."*[32] Jesus said, *"Blessed are those who hunger and thirst for righteousness, for they shall be satisfied."*[33]

May God give you a passion for Him. May He rekindle the fire of your first love and cause your heart to be hungry and thirsty for His righteousness. May He create within you such a spiritual desire for Him that you will not be satisfied with less but will press on to Him and His fullness.

What Jesus offers is more satisfying than Ye Olde 96er at Denny's Beer Barrel Pub any day!

The merciful, made merciful by mercy, find mercy in its fullness awaiting them at last.

—*F. W. Boreham*

The only thing that stands between a man and what he wants from life is often merely the will to try it and the faith to believe that it is possible.

—*Richard M. DeVos*

❖

CHAPTER SIX

The Attitude of Mercy

"Blessed are the merciful, for they shall receive mercy."
Matthew 5:7

One day a woman who occasionally walked through the park after work stopped to have her picture taken by a photographer. She was very excited to receive the immediate print-out from the digital camera; but when she looked at it, her countenance dropped. She turned to the photographer and stated rather sharply, "This is not right! This is just not right! You have done me no justice!" The man looked at the picture and then looked at her and said, "Ma'am, you don't need justice; what you need is mercy!"

That terrible joke introduces us to the fifth Beatitude found in Matthew 5:7: *"Blessed are the merciful, for they will be shown mercy."* The word blessed means much more than happiness. It has the idea of being congratulated, completed or fulfilled. If we listen carefully, we can hear the applause of heaven when we put into practice these eight character qualities or "be-attitudes."

As we understand what it means to be merciful, we transition from the first four beatitudes, which focus on our needs: we are bankrupt in spirit, and broken with grief, which leads to meekness, and an insatiable hunger for righteousness. We now move from our need, to what we need to do; from belief to behavior; from our situation to our responsibility.

Mercy Has Meaning For My Life

The word *mercy* is used approximately 250 times in the Old Testament. It is also translated as *kindness* and *loving-kindness*. When Jesus uses the word mercy, what does He mean? Mercy is an emotional response to the needs of others; it is the emotion within us that feels the pain of another so deeply that we're compelled to do something about it.

Scottish commentator William Barclay says mercy is, *"to get inside someone's skin until we can see things with his eyes, think things with his mind, and feel things with his feelings; to move in and act on behalf of those who are hurting."*[1] Mercy is an attitude.

Mercy is not something that can be turned on and off at will. Mercy, as demonstrated by Christ, involves the way a person truly feels. It is an underlying attitude toward life. Mercy is to see others as Christ sees them and feel toward others as He feels toward them. The merciful are to have an attitude of mercy toward everyone. And let's face it, we all need mercy when it comes to our relationship with God. Mercy, however, is more than just an emotion; it is also action.

When springtime arrives each year, it is not able to keep itself a secret. Spring expresses itself through blooming flowers and singing birds (along with heightened asthma and allergies!). And when the springtime of mercy is in our hearts, it makes itself known in a multitude of ways. When mercy is translated into action, we are kind and gracious in our judgment of others. We look for the best in other people. We ask ourselves: "What circumstance led this person to do wrong?" rather than, "How can I expose or punish this wrong doer?" Redemption, not condemnation, will be our concern. Mercy that is action, ministers to others. It is one thing to feel mercy—it requires an additional step to show it. Those who are merciful help lighten the load of another person.

Mercy that is action forgives others. Perhaps there is no greater expression of love than forgiveness. When you have every right to be resentful but choose to forgive, you introduce happiness that only mercy can bring.

Mercy Was Modeled For Us By Jesus

Jesus told two parables to help us understand the two sides of mercy. The first one is found in Matthew 18 and emphasizes the need to extend forgiveness because in God's mercy, He has forgiven us. The second is found in Luke 10; it is popularly known as the story of the "Good Samaritan." In this account, Jesus establishes that our feelings of compassion must be fleshed out by our actions.

In Matthew 18, we read that one day Peter approached Jesus and asked Him a question. *"Lord, how many times shall I forgive my brother when he sins against me? Up to seven times?"*[2]

Before Jesus could answer, Peter responded to his own question by suggesting that seven times would be a good limit. The rabbis taught that you were to forgive someone three times; after that you were permitted to retaliate. Peter doubled that and added an extra one for good measure. As Jesus often does, His answer to Peter was unexpected and disarming. *"I tell you, not seven times, but seventy times seven times."*[3] Seventy times seven means there is no limit to the number of times we are to forgive someone because we can't keep score when it comes to forgiveness. Mercy has about it a maddening quality because by definition it is undeserved, unmerited, and unfair.

Mercy Is Releasing The Debt

Since the concept of forgiveness without limits is hard for us to grasp, Jesus told a story to help illustrate what He meant. *"Therefore the kingdom of heaven is like a king who wanted to settle accounts with his servants. As he began the settlement, a man who owed him 10,000 talents was brought to him."*[4] The king sent out his collection agents and they came back with a man who owed the equivalent of about $25 million. Since he couldn't pay the debt, we read that, *"the master ordered that he and his wife and his children and all that he had be sold to repay the debt."*

At this point, the servant did what most of us would have done. He fell on his knees and begged, *"Have patience with me, and I will pay back everything."*[5] The king was moved. The Bible says that he was filled with compassion (that's another word for mercy). The king not only set him free, he also forgave the debt. This is exactly what mercy is all about. To extend mercy is to *cancel the debt.* The servant did not deserve this forgiveness; it was purely an act of mercy on the part of the king.

As this humbled man walked away with this wonderful gift of forgiveness, he ran into a buddy who owed him about ten bucks. Instead of canceling the debt, he grabbed his in-debt friend and began to choke him, saying, *"Pay back what you owe me!"*[6] Jesus continues the narrative by explaining that the forgiven man's friend fell to his knees and asked for patience and mercy. In fact, his plea was almost identical to the other man's when he was before the king: *"Have patience with me, and I will repay you."*[7] But, there's one big difference. Instead of forgiving the wrong out of gratitude for the forgiveness he had received, the Bible says about the one who was forgiven, *"he went off and had the man thrown in prison until he could pay the debt."*[8]

Word got around and soon everyone was talking about these incredible events. It wasn't the fact that the man would not forgive his friend that shocked them; *it was that he was so unforgiving after having found such mercy and grace himself.* The story makes its way back to the king who is justifiably angry. He sends his soldiers to bring the man he had previously forgiven before him. The king said, *"'You wicked servant. I canceled all that debt of yours because you begged me to. Shouldn't you have had mercy on your fellow servant just as I had on you?' In anger his master turned him over to the jailers to be tortured until he paid back all he owed."9*

We can be a lot like this man when we don't forgive others. We sometimes even enjoy putting people into an emotional prison when they wrong us because we want them to suffer and hurt as much as they hurt us. What happened to him will happen to each of us unless we learn to give mercy and forgive wrongs. The hidden tortures of anger and bitterness will eat our insides out as we lie awake at night stewing over every wrong that someone has committed against us. When we choose to withhold forgiveness, we are imprisoned in the past and locked out of all potential for change. Have you ever noticed that some of the most miserable people in the world are those who are unwilling to be merciful? What Lewis Smedes writes is so true: *"When I genuinely forgive, I set a prisoner free and then discover that the prisoner I set free was me."*10 Mercy is releasing the debt.

Mercy Is Restoring The Downtrodden

The first half of showing mercy is to release the debts of those who have done wrong. The second half has to do with restoring those who are downtrodden. In Luke 10, Jesus shares the parable of the Good Samaritan in response to a lawyer's question in which the doctor of jurisprudence was looking for a love loophole, a legal limit so he would know who he had to help and who he could ignore. The attorney asked, *"And who is my neighbor?"*11

Jesus answers by saying that a man went down from Jerusalem to Jericho (a distance of about 22 miles). This road wound its way through the mountains and was known as the "Bloody Way" because thieves and terrorists used it to ambush unsuspecting travelers. That's exactly what happened one day as robbers attacked a man, stripped him of his clothes and left him half-dead. This story gives us a very vivid picture of the four dimensions of mercy.

#1 Mercy Dimension: I must notice those in need.

This is always the first step. We must notice someone in need before we will do anything about meeting that need. The priest, the Levite, and the Samaritan all saw the man, but only one perceived a person in trouble: *"A priest happened to be going down the same road, and when he saw the man, he passed by on the other side. So too, a Levite, when he came to the place and saw him, passed by on the other side."*[12] Both of these religious men had come from God's presence, but somehow God's presence never got through to them. *"But a Samaritan, as he traveled, came where the man was; and when he saw him ..."*[13] This is an interesting twist because the Jews and the Samaritans hated each other. The Samaritans were considered racial and religious heretics. But the Samaritan had a notion that something was wrong and slowed down.

Erma Bombeck shares an interesting story about a time that she was waiting for a flight in an airport. She was reading a book in an effort to shut out the commotion around her:

> *A voice next to me belonging to an elderly woman said, 'I'll bet it's cold in Chicago!' Stone-faced, I replied, 'It's likely.' 'I haven't been to Chicago in three years,' she persisted. 'My son lives there.' 'That's nice,' I said, my eyes intent on my book. 'My husband's body is on this plane. We've been married 53 years ...'*

> Bombeck continues, *'I don't think I ever detested myself more than I did at that moment. Another human being was screaming to be heard and, in desperation, had turned to a cold stranger who was more interested in a novel than in the real-life drama at her elbow. She talked numbly and steadily until we boarded the plane, then found her seat in another section. As I hung up my coat, I heard her plaintive voice say to her seat companion, 'I'll bet it's cold in Chicago.'*[14]

Do you have any notion of the needs around you? Here's a simple prayer that will help you: *"Lord, let me see people through Your eyes."*

#2 Mercy Dimension: I must feel the pain of others intensely.

All three passers-by saw the need, but only the Samaritan felt the need: *"he took pity on him."*[15] The word pity means to have intensity in the intestines. Someone put it this way: *"Mercy begins when your hurt comes into my heart."* The Samaritan was shaken up when he saw the man who was beaten down.

#3 Mercy Dimension: I must go to the person in need.

The Samaritan saw the need, felt for the man, and then went into action: *"he went to him ..."*[16] True mercy always involves motion. One pastor wrote,

> *"I was walking down the streets of a town; and as I looked over toward a doorway, I noticed a derelict lying on the ground. Sand and old newspapers were blowing up around his body. He had passed out. He was just lying there. All up and down that busy street, well-dressed people were walking, going about their business. Many of them looked down at that piece of humanity on the ground, but nobody stopped to help. Nobody did anything. After we had gone to dinner and come back, that man was still lying there. I could not believe that nobody had done anything."* [17]

Religious people today still miss seeing the needs of people through God's eyes.

Some of us see needs and move on while shaking our heads and clicking our tongues. Others of us feel badly for those in pain. Only those who move to meet needs are demonstrating mercy.

#4 Mercy Dimension: I must act as the feet and hands of mercy.

When the Samaritan comprehended that something was wrong, he was moved in his emotions, he went into motion, and then he demonstrated mercy as he bandaged the man's wounds, put him on his own donkey (which meant he had to walk), took him to an inn, and took care of him. The next day, he gave the innkeeper two silver coins, which represented two days' wages in the first century. He even promised to come back and take care of any extra expenses. Do you see the difference in those two questions? The first question focuses on the claim that others have on my time and resources. The second question reframes reality to what I owe to the suffering people all around me. The issue is one of character, not of criteria; about being a neighbor, not defining a neighbor. In answering Jesus' query regarding who acted as a neighbor in this story, the lawyer correctly answered, *"The one who had mercy on him."* Jesus then tells him, and us, *"Go, and do likewise."*[18]

Catherine Booth was the "mother" of the Salvation Army. *"Wherever Catherine Booth went,"* said G. Campbell Morgan, *"humanity went to hear her. Princes and peeresses merged with paupers and prostitutes."* One night, Morgan shared in a meeting with Mrs. Booth; a great crowd of "publicans and sinners" were there. Her message brought many to Christ.

After the meeting, Morgan and Mrs. Booth went to be entertained at a fine home; and the lady of the manor said, "My dear Mrs. Booth, that meeting was dreadful."

"What do you mean, dear?" asked Mrs. Booth.

"Oh, when you were speaking, I was looking at those people opposite to me. Their faces were so terrible, many of them. I don't think I shall sleep tonight!"

"Why, dearie, don't you know them?" Mrs. Booth asked; and the hostess replied, "Certainly not!"

"Well, that is interesting," Mrs. Booth said. "I did not bring them with me from London; they are your neighbors!" Your neighbor is anyone in need. You are a neighbor when you minister mercy to the downtrodden. Will you walk on by? Start with the need that is near you, and you'll be reminded of the nearness of Jesus in your own life. *Mercy always demands that we do something.*

We could say it this way: *Mercy embraces both forgiveness for the guilty and compassion for the suffering.*

Mercy Is To Be A Regular Part Of My Daily Life

"Blessed are the merciful." How can we become merciful? If you're anything like me—and my guess is that you are—I often find it so easy to judge, criticize, and condemn. How can we change and become people who demonstrate mercy? Remember that as Christians, we are people who have received mercy.

We often make mistakes that require God's mercy, so we should be merciful to others. Paul reminds us to watch our own actions when we become aware of another who is caught in a sin: *"If someone falls into sin, forgivingly restore him, saving your critical comments for yourself. You might be needing forgiveness before the day's out."*[19]

One of Aesop's most popular fables is called, "The Lion and the Mouse."

> *Once when a Lion was asleep, a little Mouse began running up and down upon him; this soon wakened the Lion, who placed his huge paw upon him, and opened his big jaws to swallow him.*
>
> *"Pardon, O King," cried the little Mouse, "forgive me this time, I shall never forget it. Who knows but I may be able to do you a turn some of these days?"*
>
> *The Lion was so tickled at the idea of the Mouse being able to help him that he lifted up his paw and let him go. Some time later, hunters who desired to carry him alive to the King, tied the Lion to a tree while they went in search of a wagon on which to carry him. Just then the little Mouse happened to pass by, and seeing the sad plight in which the*

Lion was, went up to him and soon gnawed away the ropes that bound the King of the Beasts.

"Was I not right?" said the little Mouse.

One of the morals of the story is that little friends may prove great friends. Become acquainted with someone that you are inclined to judge. Chances are that you really do not know that person very well. The word *prejudice* means to pre-judge or to make an estimate of someone else without knowing all the facts. We frequently do this without knowing the person at all.

Television shows such as *Dateline* or *48 Hours* ask us to form an opinion based on a ten-minute interview and heavily-biased voiceovers. It is easy to be unrelenting in our judgment of those we do not know; we need, therefore, to become better acquainted with backgrounds of others and seek to understand the problems they face and the reason for the scars on their souls.

Allow Jesus To Show His Mercy Through You

To the believers in Colosse, Paul wrote, *"... Christ in you, the hope of glory."* [20] What an affirmation! And Christ in you is your only hope of becoming a loving, merciful person. As you surrender your bitterness and resentment to Jesus and allow Him to live and work freely through you, mercy becomes a normal attitude of life.

Who do you need to release from debt today? Forgiveness is the virtue we most enjoy but least employ. Nothing proves more clearly that we have been recipients of mercy than our own readiness to forgive.

What downtrodden person can you restore this week? You don't necessarily have to go looking for someone; God will bring the person along your path. What will you do? Will you be a taker, a keeper, or a giver?

When Frederick II, King of Prussia (1712-86), known for his corrosive and icy wit, went on an inspection tour of a prison, he was greeted with the cries of prisoners, most of whom fell on their knees, loudly protesting their unjust punishment. While listening to these pleas of innocence, the King's eye was caught by a solitary figure in the corner, a prisoner seemingly unconcerned with all the commotion. King Frederick called out to him, *"Why are you here?"*

The prisoner replied, *"Armed robbery, your Majesty."* The king then asked, *"Were you guilty?"* To which the prisoner answered, *"Oh yes, indeed, your Majesty. I entirely deserve my punishment."*

At that, Frederick commanded the jailer: *"Release this guilty man at once. I will not have him kept in this prison where he will corrupt all the fine innocent people who occupy it."*

We're all guilty. And the sooner we admit it, the better off we'll be. When God takes our picture, we don't want justice; we cry out for mercy. And it is the consistent teaching of the New Testament that, indeed, only the merciful shall receive mercy.[21]

Goldilocks said a good thing on Sunday night. She was squatting on the hearthrug in her nightdress, learning the Beatitudes for her teacher.

"Well," I said, when she closed her Bible. "Which do you like best?"

"Oh, the sixth!" she replied at once.

"And why?"

"Because, if I were pure in heart, I should have all the other virtues as well!"

—*F. W. Boreham*

❖

CHAPTER SEVEN

The Attitude of Purity

"Blessed are the pure in heart, for they shall see God."
Matthew 5:8

When I was younger—in a slightly more innocent age—I used to dress up for Halloween. The ultimate costume for me was Batman. (And no—it wasn't because of the tights!) It was the cape, the mysterious black and grey color combination and the *piece de résistance!*—the mask. I loved the thought that once in costume, no one—not even my mother, would recognize me. I could fight crime, battle evil characters (who obviously possessed enough loonies to keep a team of psychiatrists in business for quite a long time), save damsels in distress, drive a really cool car, live in a cave, and be home in time for supper.

Maybe you can relate, but we've aged and left childish fantasies behind. Only the masks have changed.

We all wear masks from time to time. We pretend to be someone or something we're not so that others will accept or admire us. The mask is usually vastly different from who we really are.

In the fantasy world of a six or seven-year-old boy, it's okay to wear a Batman mask. But why do we continue to don masks when we've reached adulthood? Maybe it's because we're afraid to be ourselves, so we pretend to be someone else. Many of us try to be cool and confident when we really aren't. Some of us try to kiss up to authority figures—teachers, parents, bosses—when it's really just an act. At church, you'll probably find some people who pretend to be more devout than they really are—as if God doesn't know!

We desperately try to fit in: through sports, the clothing we wear, or the car we drive. Sometimes we make choices just so people will like us more. Some of us paste on a smile so that folks will not notice the person behind the smile. We want others to like us because sometimes we don't like ourselves.

Hiding who you really are before God and others is like putting a piece of pizza under your bed. Others in your home probably don't know it's there, but then they start to smell it. You might succeed in hiding who you really are from some people for a while, but eventually they'll figure you out. Others will catch a whiff sooner or later.

Jesus speaks to us about the feelings we have when we want to hide or pretend to be someone or something we really aren't. He reminds us that His desire is for us to be honest, and that honesty will compel us to be like Him. To be like Him means to live a life of purity. *"Blessed are the pure in heart for they shall see God."*

Let's examine what Jesus is teaching us through this particular beatitude.

The Meaning Of Purity

What exactly does it mean to be pure in heart? The term *heart* is a metaphor of the inner person. The word *heart* comes from the Greek word *kardia* from which we get our English word *cardiac*.

Similar words are used in many cultures to refer to the inner person, the seat of motives and attitudes, or the center of the personality. In some societies, they use *kidneys* or *bowels*. (Imagine singing, *"I Left My Bowels in San Francisco"* or *"Deep in the Kidneys of Texas"*!)

In the Bible, the heart not only represents the deepest emotions and feelings, it also represents the mind and the will. Proverbs says, *"As a man thinks in his heart, so is he."*[1] In Matthew, Jesus asked some scribes, "Why do you entertain evil thoughts in your hearts?"[2]

God has always been more concerned with the inside of us; He's infinitely more concerned with our hearts than anything else. Let's check out a few Bible verses which drive home the point:

- Proverbs says, *"Watch over your heart with all diligence, for from it flows the springs of life."*[3]

- God sent the Flood because He *"saw that the wickedness of man was great in the earth, and that every intent of the thoughts of his heart was only evil continually."*[4]

- After committing adultery, David prayed, *"Create in me a clean heart, O God."*[5]

- The Psalmist Asaph wrote, *"Truly God is good to Israel, to such as are pure in heart."*[6]

- Jeremiah said, *"The heart is deceitful above all things, and desperately wicked; who can know it? I, the LORD, search the heart."*[7]

- Jesus Himself said, *"For from the heart come evil thoughts, murder, adultery, all other sexual immorality, theft, lying, and slander."*[8]

To live as a "pure in heart person" demands that I deal with my inner life.

Pure in heart is also a term that is a synonym of holiness. "Pure" translates from *katharos*, the word from which we get *catharsis*. Catharsis is a term used in psychology and counseling that refers to a cleansing of the mind or emotions. The Greek word for pure leads us to understand that something is being cleansed from dirt, filth, or contamination. In classical Greek, the word was most often used to describe metals that had been refined in the fire until they were pure—free from impurities. Jesus wants us to have a pure, clean, unmasked heart.

Let's put these two definitions together. *A person with a passion for purity is one who has been cleansed in character so that the way he or she looks in public is the way he or she is in private.*

You've heard it said, *"Character is what you are when no one is looking."* The one who is single-minded in his commitment to Christ will also be inwardly pure. *"Who may ascend the hill of the LORD? Who may stand in His holy place? He who has clean hands and a pure heart, who does not lift up his soul to an idol or swear by what is false."*[9]

What Is The Benefit Of Being Pure In Heart?

Benefit #1: I will be blessed.

The first word of this beatitude says we will be "blessed." The word means "happy," "fortunate," or "congratulations." Earlier in Chapter Two, we defined what it means to be blessed as Jesus uses the word. If you want to be blessed and fulfilled, become *"pure in heart."*

Benefit #2: I will see God.

A second benefit of being *"pure in heart"* is that we will *"see God."* Don't misunderstand; we are not ready to see God with physical eyes.

Moses was serving as the leader of Israel when God delivered them from slavery in Egypt. Moses is also known as the Lawgiver because He climbed high on Mt. Sinai to receive the law from God. His relationship with God was unique in human history.

In Exodus 33, while talking with God on a mountaintop, Moses voiced one of his heart's deepest desires, *"Please, show me Your glory."*[10] God replied, *"You cannot see My face; for no man shall see Me, and live."*[11] However, God did allow Moses to see His back, but the LORD said, *"My face shall not be seen."*[12]

Why couldn't Moses see God's face? He wasn't ready. Though he was a man full of faith who walked with God with a pure heart few have ever known, Moses still lived in his sinful flesh. We will not see the face of God until that great day when our sinful flesh is gone, and we stand before Him in glorified bodies.

The apostle John wrote, *"Beloved, now we are children of God; and it has not yet been revealed what we shall be, but we know that when He is revealed, we shall be like Him, for we shall see Him as He is."*[13]

Benefit #3: I can see God with spiritual eyes in the present.

Jesus said, *"If you have seen me, you have seen the Father."*[14]

I recently read of a young girl who asked a lady in her church, *"Why do you close your eyes when you sing?"* She replied, *"So I can see God."* When we shut out the distractions of the world and focus on purity, we see God at work all around us.

If you will look around, you may very well "see" God in your family, your church, your small group, your relationships with others, and even at your place of employment.

One of the greatest characteristics of Jesus is that, unlike us, He never wore a mask. He is totally genuine. He never hides anything because He has nothing to hide. He calls us to join Him, to take off the masks, because He has made us "pure in heart."

One day a young minister was being escorted through a coal mine. At the entrance he saw a beautiful white flower growing out of the black earth. *"How can it blossom in such purity and radiance in this dirty mine?"* the preacher asked. *"Throw some coal dust on it, and see for yourself,"* his guide replied. When the minister did just that, he was surprised to observe that the fine, sooty coal particles slid right off the snowy petals, leaving the plant just as lovely and unstained as before. Its surface was so smooth that the grit and grime could not adhere to it. If we know Christ as our Savior and live each day surrendered to Him, the grime and dirt of the world will slide right off. Throw away your mask and be genuine before Him.

The Pathway To Purity

Let's take a look at a true-to-life story found in 2 Samuel 11. It's a story regarding King David, the man whom the apostle Paul tells us was a man after God's own heart.[15] Yet here we find one of the greatest heroes of the Bible wearing a mask.

It's a familiar story. We find King David up on his rooftop. Roofs back then were flat, and often people slept on the roof when the night was warm in order to be refreshed by any evening breezes. While he was up there, David saw a beautiful woman bathing. He desired her. After inquiring about her, he learned she was the wife of one of the soldiers in his army. Did that stop his lust? No—what a king wants, a king gets. He sent for her, she arrived to greet her king and he slept with her. David might have been thinking, "It's good to be the king!"

David, however, committed serious errors on several counts. First, he had sexual relations with a woman to whom he was not married. God clearly says that is sinful. Second, he took the wife of another man. He was violating *their* marriage covenant. Third, he used his power as king to make this happen. There is no hint that the woman, Bathsheba, wanted this. David was abusing his royal authority, the authority that God had given him.

As the story unfolds, it becomes even more interesting. I'll bet you can guess what happens next. Yep: Bathsheba discovers that she is pregnant with David's baby.

Suddenly, what was a private sin, consummated in the throes of passion on a hot summer night, was about to become very, very public. Bathsheba was married to a soldier named Uriah. When Uriah came home from war in a few months and found his wife pregnant, he would know the child wasn't his. When this story broke, everyone would know David wasn't the godly spiritual leader he claimed to be. He was wearing a mask. David obviously didn't want this unpleasant truth to get out, so he planned his cover-up. First, he summoned Uriah home from the front.

*So David sent this word to Joab: 'Send me Uriah the
Hittite.' And Joab sent him to David. When Uriah came to
him, David asked him how Joab was, how the soldiers were,
and how the war was going. Then David said to Uriah, 'Go
down to your house and wash your feet.' So Uriah left the
palace, and a gift from the king was sent after him.*[16]

David wants this warrior to come home—he's been on the
front lines for quite a while—and sleep with his wife, Bathsheba.
What man, after the rigors of soldiering, could pass that up?
When the child is born, no one, especially Uriah, will think
anything is amiss.

However, another problem emerges. Uriah is a good and loyal
soldier. He sleeps outside the palace because he can't imagine
enjoying the comforts of home while his compatriots are fighting a
war. Uriah said to David, *"The ark and Israel and Judah are staying
in tents, and my master Joab and my lord's men are camped in the open
fields. How could I go to my house to eat and drink and lie with my
wife? As surely as you live, I will not do such a thing!"*[17]

Only momentarily stymied, David concocts another plan.
After inviting Uriah to a meal, David gets him drunk and tries
his plan again. Pretty ingenious, don't you think? Surely it will
work this time! Does David's cover-up work? Nope. Uriah sleeps
outside the palace again.

David's scheme was failing, so he resorted to extreme measures.
He wrote a message to Joab, the general of David's army.

*So the next morning David wrote a letter to Joab and gave
it to Uriah to deliver. The letter instructed Joab, 'Station
Uriah on the frontlines where the battle is fiercest. Then
pull back so that he will be killed.' So Joab assigned Uriah
to a spot close to the city wall where he knew the enemy's
strongest men were fighting.*[18]

David wanted Uriah on the front line, and then left alone to fight. Surely he'd be killed and this problem would go away. And that's exactly what happened ... almost.

David's mask was one of holiness and one of leadership. What kind of masks do you wear? There are four common masks we often wear:

- *There is the holy mask.* We pretend to be more spiritual than we really are.

- *There is the well-behaved mask.* We usually wear this mask in the presence of parents, teachers, or employers. We want them to think that they will never have a problem with us. "I'll be a model of a good employee or a good kid." With this mask on we pretend to be who or what we're not.

- *There is the rebellious mask.* Usually we wear this mask when around certain friends or acquaintances. When we wear it, we're disrespectful, and we speak ill of other people, often with disdaining laughter. "I'm tough, I'm bad. If I go out for a drink with the boys or the girls, this is the mask I sometimes wear."

- *There is the "I've got it all together" mask.* When we wear this mask we pretend to be cool, confident, in control, and in touch with all the latest and greatest that's going in fashion and life and lingo. Maybe you really do have it all together, but more likely you're like me: just as dorky as everyone else; and at times, you feel pretty insecure about yourself.

Following the front-line battle, Uriah's lifeless body was brought back to camp and interred. David had committed at least two sins: adultery with Bathsheba and the murder of her husband, Uriah. David's lust led him into the first sin. What led him into the second sin? He was trying to cover up his first sin.

It seemed as if David had gotten away with it. Near the end of the chapter, in 2 Samuel 11, David's reputation was secure; he had a beautiful new wife named Bathsheba, and a bouncing baby boy. All's well that ends well, right? Very wrong! The last line of the chapter tells us, *"But the thing David had done displeased the Lord."*[19]

David had been wearing the mask of the righteous king, the psalm-writing spiritual leader, the war hero blessed by God. But God saw through the masks and sent a prophet called Nathan to confront David with a fictional vignette:

> *There were two men in a certain town. One was rich, and one was poor. The rich man owned many sheep and cattle. The poor man owned nothing but a little lamb he had worked hard to buy. He raised that little lamb, and it grew up with his children. It ate from the man's own plate and drank from his cup. He cuddled it in his arms like a baby daughter. One day a guest arrived at the home of the rich man. But instead of killing a lamb from his own flocks for food, he took the poor man's lamb and killed it and served it to his guest.*[20]

David was the rich man; Uriah the poor man. David had taken Uriah's wife from him and then insured that he would be killed in battle. When David heard this story, he was outraged! This was an injustice, and he wanted it set right. (David didn't get the point right away.) Nathan then confronted him with the famous line: *"You are the man!"*[21]

Four words changed David's life. He realized he was the rich jerk who had taken the poor man's most precious treasure. I wonder how David felt. How do you feel when your sin has been confronted? Maybe David wanted to deny it all. He might have been angry at Nathan. He might have felt an emptiness in his gut knowing the game was up—his secret machinations exposed. He might have felt some relief that he no longer had to keep this horrible secret. He certainly felt guilty for what he had done, and he was sorrowful about the consequences.

Through Nathan, God told David about the consequences of his sin: how there would be turmoil in his family, someone close to him would embarrass him before the nation, and the baby born to Bathsheba would die in infancy. All of these things came to pass.

David's response was one of honesty: *"I have sinned against the Lord."*[22]

This story teaches us many things. Let me point out just two. The first one is pretty simple: sin is bad. That's no surprise. When you go against God and His ways, you lose—every time. The second lesson is this: David's attempt at a cover-up got him deeper and deeper into sin—leading all the way to murder. The same thing happens today. A woman becomes pregnant and has an abortion so no one will know she's been sexually active. Then she carries that painful burden for the rest of her life.

Maybe after a surgical procedure, your doctors rightly prescribed pain medicine. The scars from the operation heal, the pain goes away, but you are not able to put the pain medication aside. Suddenly, you're hooked. And you're in bondage.

A dating couple justify being sexually involved with one another assuming it's okay because, "we're eventually going to get married." And they end up in an unhealthy relationship or even deeper sexual sin.

Possibly someone at work is giving you flattering attention that you're not getting at home. You're hiding behind the mask of a good marriage; all the while you're entertaining thoughts of, "I wonder what it would be like if ...?"

How do we move away from sin, bondage and pain? How do we place ourselves on the path to purity? We do what David did.

Step #1: Be Honest With Yourself

In his book, *Integrity,* Ted Engstrom relates this story:

For Coach Cleveland Stroud and the Bulldogs of Rockdale County High School (Conyers, Georgia), it was their championship season: 21 wins and 5 losses on the way to the Georgia boys' basketball tournament last March, then a dramatic come-from-behind victory in the state finals. But now the new glass trophy case outside the high school gymnasium is bare. Earlier this month the Georgia High School Association deprived Rockdale County of the championship after school officials said that a player who was scholastically ineligible had played 45 seconds in the first of the school's five post-season games. 'We didn't know he was ineligible at the time; we didn't know it until a few weeks ago,' Mr. Stroud said. 'Some people have said we should have just kept quiet about it, that it was just 45 seconds; and the player wasn't an impact player. But you've got to do what's honest and right and what the rules say. I told my team that people forget the scores of basketball games; they don't ever forget what you're made of.' [23]

Coach Stroud understood a principle that is absolutely essential to us if we are to be the men and women God desires us to be: personal honesty and integrity.

Step #2: Be Honest With God

I recall reading about a couple from Bakersfield, California, who had just purchased a new boat but were having some serious problems. They were newcomers to boating, but no matter how hard they tried, they couldn't get their 22-foot boat to run properly in the water. The motor seemed very sluggish no matter which way they turned, and no matter how much power was applied. After a frustrating hour of trying to get their boat to go, they slowly made their way to a nearby marina, hoping someone there could tell them what was wrong. A thorough check on the topside of the boat revealed that everything was in perfect working condition. The engine ran fine, the out-board motor went up and down, and the propeller was the correct size and pitch. Then, one of the marina workers jumped in the water to check underneath. He came up choking on water because he was laughing so hard. As far as I know, this is a true story: Under the boat, still strapped securely in place, was the trailer!

When God looks underneath your life, what does He see? When He looks behind your mask, what does He discover? Is your heart undivided? Or, are you strapped to some sin that is slowly pulling you under?

A Pure Life Leads to Seeing God

Following the tragic events in David's life, he took some time to collect his thoughts and write down words that have been helpful to generations of men and women. We know it as Psalm 51:

> *For the director of music. A psalm of David. When the prophet Nathan came to him after David had commit-ted adultery with Bathsheba. Have mercy on me, O God, according to Your unfailing love; according to Your great compassion blot out my transgressions. Wash away all my iniquity and cleanse me from my sin. For I know my transgressions, and my sin is always before me.*
>
> *Against You, You only, have I sinned and done what is evil in Your sight, so that You are proved right when You speak and justified when You judge.*
>
> *Cleanse me with hyssop, and I will be clean; wash me, and I will be whiter than snow. Let me hear joy and gladness; let the bones You have crushed rejoice. Hide Your face from my sins and blot out all my iniquity. Create in me a pure heart, O God, and renew a steadfast spirit within me.*[24]

David brought his heart back around to a place of purity.

The last portion of this beatitude contains Christ's promise: *"... for they will see God."* God reserves intimate fellowship with Himself for those who are unmixed in their devotion and unmasked in their relationship with Him. The nearer we approach purity of heart, the surer we become of God. The closer we get to God, the purer we will become. In our heart of hearts, above all things, we want to see Him. The writer of Ecclesiastes declares that God has put eternity in the human heart.[25] Blaise Pascal wrote about the "God-shaped vacuum" inside each of us. Augustine said that our hearts are restless until they find their rest in God. Christian history scholar Paul Thigpen wrote:

> *Unfortunately sin has blinded us, leaving our spiritual eyes swollen shut. Unable to see God, we grope in the darkness, searching desperately for someone or something to make us happy ... our heart is splintered and scattered. We run to and fro, gathering first this trinket, then that one, dropping both for the next shiny one we spy ... the result is a civil war of the soul. All the while our Father stands close by, waiting for us to turn around and run into His arms ... if our vision of God is to grow wider, clearer, and brighter, our will must be united in a single focus on Him and an overriding desire to know and love Him.[26]*

Are you ready to see God like you never have before? Is your desire to know Him as intense as David's when he wrote, *"I have sought your face with all my heart; be gracious to me according to your promise"?* [27] If so, then it's time to cut loose anything that is keeping you from moving forward.

It's time to end the cover-up and begin the clean-up —and only God can do that kind of cleansing. When you want to remove the mask, go to Psalm 51. Memorize it. Because when you're tired of playing games, this Psalm will lead you back to the God who knows you better than you know yourself.

The idea is a very simple and a very familiar one. We meet a young fellow in the street. All at once, some little mannerism, some inflection of the voice, some movement of the hand, some expression of the face, recalls the memory of an old friend. Is it possible? Is this his son? We inquire and quickly find that our suspicion is well-founded. That is precisely the idea of the seventh beatitude. The world will see in the peacemaker a softened, hallowed mirroring of the divine glory.

—*F. W. Boreham*

❖

CHAPTER EIGHT

The Attitude of Conciliation

"Blessed are the peacemakers, for they will be called sons of God."
Matthew 5:9

As I write this, I sit before an open window listening to the rushing sound of a trout stream just outside. The verdant North Carolina hills surround me. From this perch, one would never suspect that America is at war on two fronts: Afghanistan and Iraq. Personal friends and acquaintances of mine are serving overseas in the United States military, placing their lives in jeopardy. Seemingly, everyone I speak with about the war, knows someone fighting it. We're not immune to conflict. It's everywhere, the world over.

Years ago, a large statue of Christ was erected high in the Andes Mountains on the border between Argentina and Chile. The statue, called "Christ of the Andes," symbolizes a pledge between the two countries that as long as it stands, there will be peace between them.

Shortly after the statue was erected, the Chileans began to protest that they had been slighted—the statue of Christ had its back turned to Chile. Just when tempers were at their highest, a Chilean newspaperman saved the day. In an editorial that not only satisfied the people but made them laugh, he simply said, "The people of Argentina need more watching over than the Chileans!" [1]

We chuckle at that because underlying the humor is the truth that all of us are predisposed to conflict. In fact, some of us have clashed with so many people, that we don't really know how to live peaceably with others. I've known some individuals over the years that never seem happy unless they are fighting with someone.

I enjoy the story of a young daughter who was working so diligently on her homework that her father became curious and asked her what she was doing. She looked up at her dad and replied, *"I'm writing a report on how to bring peace to the world."* The father smiled and said, *"Isn't that a pretty big order for a little girl?"* The school girl continued writing as she answered, *"Oh, no. Don't worry. There are three of us in the class working on it."*

It's easy to be naïve about peace. In fact, however, it is very elusive in our churches, relationships, and cultures. I recently heard about a group of people who were walking across America on a mission of peace. Unfortunately, they couldn't get along and divided into two groups in Arkansas! That reminds me of what one person said about Christians who quarrel: *"Where two or three come together in Jesus' name ... there will eventually be conflict."*

The fact that the lack of peace is so pervasive is really nothing new. We can trace it back to the early chapters of Genesis. Humans have been at war with God ever since Adam and Eve sinned. And, initiated by the conflict between Cain and Abel, which eventually led to one brother killing the other, we have been in a bombastic battle with our brothers and sisters right up to the present.

In the midst of this continuous conflict and incessant strife, Jesus speaks some stunning words in this beatitude. *"Blessed are the peacemakers, for they will be called sons of God."*[2] Eugene Peterson, in his paraphrase, puts it this way: *"You're blessed when you can show people how to cooperate instead of compete or fight. That's when you discover who you really are and your place in God's family."*[3]

As we discovered in our previous chapter, we are to be pure before God. This present beatitude challenges us to be at peace with others. Let me remind you that Jesus is not listing some optional ideas or preaching a sermon with some suggestions we might want to consider. These eight beatitudes are meant to describe the disciple of Christ and set forth the blessings that come to those who follow Him wholeheartedly. Christ begins by introducing the concept of peace. We all desire it, yet find it elusive. In our search then, we had better understand what peace is not and what peace is. Peace is not simply the absence of activity. We often use the phrase "peace and quiet" to refer to our need to slow down. Yet we find ourselves living in a hectic culture whose mantra seems to be, "Honk if you love peace and quiet!" And who among us, because of a jam-packed schedule, hasn't desired a vacation following our vacation?

Peace is also more than the absence of hostility. The biblical concept is much deeper than just not having conflict. Peace is not just getting away from reality.

Peace is not just the absence of something; rather, it is the presence of something: harmony and unity. The Bible is a book of peace; the word "peace" appears over 400 times in Scripture, with many other indirect references. Scripture refers to God as the *"God of peace,"*[4] and because this is part of His very character, He wants His people to be marked by peace as well. Jesus is also described by Isaiah in the Old Testament as the *"Prince of Peace."*[5]

In the Old Testament, the word peace is *shalom*. Peace, as a Hebrew concept, is to be understood as a state of wholeness and harmony that is intended to resonate in all of our relationships. When used as a greeting, *shalom* is a wish for outward freedom from disturbance as well as an inward sense of well-being. To the Jews, a people constantly harassed by enemies, peace was the premiere blessing. God gave Moses the following words to use when blessing His people: *"The Lord bless you and keep you; the Lord make His face shine upon you and be gracious to you; the Lord turn His face toward you and give you peace."*[6] Every one of Paul's thirteen letters begins with a greeting of peace. Some of them also end with words of peace. Since peace is such an important theme throughout Scripture and Jesus calls His followers to be peacemakers, we need to understand what He meant.

What Is A Peacemaker?

The only place the word *peacemaker* occurs in the Scripture is in the fifth chapter of Matthew. We also have what seems to be a reflection of this truth in the epistle penned by James: *"Peacemakers who sow in peace raise a harvest of righteousness."*[7]

In Jesus' day, a peacemaker was an ambassador sent to bring a treaty of peace. The word He employs here would, perhaps, be better rendered *peace-workers*, implying not merely making peace between those who are at odds, but promoting peace between the two opposing parties. Thus bringing about the will of God in their lives.[8]

We have an incredible example of this type of peacemaker in the Old Testament, personified in a woman by the name of Abigail. Let's look at her story and extract some principles that are true of every person who desires to be a peacemaker.

Abigail was married to a man called Nabal (whose name literally is translated "fool"), and she apparently was an Old Testament babe! She was one of the six Old Testament beauties, along with Sarai,[9] Rachel,[10] Tamar,[11] Abishag,[12] and Esther.[13] We're told that she was more outstanding than any of the other biblical beauties. Abigail has been described to us as one who was not only beautiful in her appearance, but she was a beauty with brains.

Abigail is the only woman in the Bible praised for her intelligence and beauty in the same sentence. The Bible notes her first for her intelligence and then for her beauty. She had something money cannot buy, makeup cannot provide, men cannot repress, and something more powerful than muscles, bodyguards, and weapons: she had brains. She was smart in the head, swift on her feet, and sharp with her words.

As we review the following story from her life, we find that her story is interwoven with David's life, while impacting the life of her foolish husband, Nabal. There is much we can learn from

Abigail. By her life, we learn what we need to do as we assume our role of peacemakers.

God Can Use Me To Make Peace

In 1 Samuel 25, we are presented with the account of Abigail's prudent management for the preserving of her husband and family from the destruction that was unknowingly coming upon them; and we find that she did her part admirably well.

Here's the *Reader's Digest* version of what happened: Nabal was a very wealthy man, rich in lands and livestock. David was traveling through the desert with his band of men. It was sheep-shearing time (more on that later). Earlier David had come across some of Nabal's shepherds and treated them with customary courtesy and respect. David and his men were hungry and on the move. He sent ten men to Nabal, who brought him greetings of good health and long life. They asked that, since Nabal's shepherds had received civil treatment from David, could Nabal find it in his heart to offer these men food and drink?

Nabal responded that he had neither heard of David, nor these men. Who might they be anyway? He had enough to worry about without bothering with the likes of a nomadic, sheep-herding band of miscreants. The men returned to David, apprising him of Nabal's response. David, to put it mildly, did not receive this news well. He had 400 of his men put on their swords and began riding to confront Nabal. Word came to Abigail through a servant of what was underway, and she immediately sprang into action.

It is hard to say whether Abigail was more miserable with such a husband or Nabal happy with such a wife. She headed David off at the pass. As she approached David regarding her husband, we find that she may have come with some intended humor, playing off the pun of his name. She almost seems to be asking, "What can you expect from one with such a name?"

Proverbs teaches us that a virtuous woman is a crown to her husband, to protect him as well as adorn him, and will do him good and not evil.[14] Wisdom, in such a case as this, was better than beauty or weapons of war. By her very actions and sagacity, Abigail teaches us the characteristics of a peacemaker. Let's sit at her feet and learn from her.

A peacemaker doesn't waste time.

"Then Abigail hurried."[15] It was her wisdom that guided her to what she did; she did it quickly and without delay; she put the pedal to the metal! It was no time to trifle or linger; everything was suddenly in danger. If we desire peace in our lives, we must spring into action as soon as possible. David and his men were on their way to have it out with Nabal; but before they arrived, Abigail went to meet them halfway.

Jesus spoke about this kind of wisdom and foresight in the context of counting the cost of discipleship. He asked, *"... what king, when he sets out to meet another king in battle, will not first sit down and take counsel whether or not he is strong enough with ten thousand men to encounter the one coming against him with twenty thousand? Or else, while the other is still far away, he sends a delegation and asks terms of peace"* [underline mine].[16]

A peacemaker doesn't wait for someone else to step in.

Abigail's wisdom demanded that action be taken, because being a person of great prudence and wisdom, she knew better how to manage the situation than any of her servants. The Bible says, *"As she came riding her donkey into a mountain ravine, there were David and his men descending toward her, and she met them."*[17]

The peacemaker always takes the initiative, not waiting for someone else to come along to be the peacemaker. A peacemaker recognizes what needs to be done, when it needs to be done, and intuitively realizes, "I'm the person God has placed in this situation for such a time as this."

Abigail—in order to stave off disaster upon her family—made it her responsibility to atone for Nabal's faults. We must assess and understand Nabal's actions in light of the culture of the time. Hospitality was and is a social obligation in the East; Jesus had sharp words for a person whose hospitality was mean and grudging:

> *"... he [Jesus] said to Simon, 'Do you see this woman? I entered your house, you gave Me no water for My feet, but she has washed My feet with her tears, and wiped them with the hair of her head. You gave Me no kiss, but this woman has not ceased to kiss My feet since the time I came in. You did not anoint My head with oil, but this woman has anointed my feet with fragrant oil ...'"*[18]

It was sheep-shearing time, similar to our harvest season; a time when generosity and giving were the order of the day, as it is at Christmastime in our country. Nabal was denying David's men the normal conventions of the day. He had been rude to David's messengers in two ways, and by that, he had been rude to David: he had denied David's men the provisions they asked for, and he had done so with unkind, provoking language.

A peacemaker comes humbly.

> *"When Abigail saw David, she quickly got off her donkey and bowed down before David with her face to the ground. She fell at his feet and said: 'My lord, let the blame be on me alone. Please let your servant speak to you; hear what your servant has to say.'"*[19]

With a humble, obliging demeanor, and with charming speech, she began to atone for the abusive language which Nabal had used against them. She met David upon the march, his heart filled with rage and resentment; meditating the destruction of Nabal; but with every expression of respect at her disposal, she begs his favor, and entreats him to allow the offense to go. Her demeanor was very submissive: *"[She] fell on her face before David, and bowed herself to the ground."*[20]

The yielded spirit and humble heart of the peacemaker can pacify the one who has been greatly offended. Abigail placed herself into the posture of a penitent person. She was not ashamed to do it; it was for the good of her home and children. She assumed this posture in the sight of both her own servants and David's soldiers. She humbly begged David to give her a hearing: *"... please let your maidservant speak to you."*[21] As she began her defense, every statement was well-placed and well-expressed.

A peacemaker gives a gift.

By giving a generous present, Abigail atoned for Nabal's denial of the appropriate request David's men had made. *"She took two hundred loaves of bread, two skins of wine, five dressed sheep, five seahs of roasted grain, a hundred cakes of raisins and two hundred cakes of pressed figs, and loaded them on donkeys."*[22]

If Nabal had given David's men what he should have, they would have gone away thankful; but Abigail prepared the very best her house could afford and gave them an abundance of it, according to the usual entertainments of those times; not only *bread* and *meat*, but *raisins* and *figs* also. Nabal refused them *water*, but she took *two casks of wine*, loaded her donkeys with these provisions, and sent them ahead. We gain great wisdom from the writer of Proverbs when we read, *"A quietly given gift soothes an irritable person; a heartfelt present cools a hot temper."*[23]

Abigail not only rightfully, but laudably, disposed all of these goods of her husband's without his knowledge (even when she had reason to think that if he had known what she did, he would not have consented to it), because it was not to gratify her own pride or vanity, but for the necessary defense of her husband and her family, which otherwise would have been inevitably ruined.

In presenting the gifts, she wisely says, *"And let this gift, which your servant has brought to my master, be given to the men who follow you."*[24] She gives the presents she had brought, but speaks of them as unworthy of David's acceptance, and therefore desires that they be given to the young men who had been offended and so rudely treated.

A peacemaker has a generous spirit.

Abigail continues, *"Please forgive your servant's offense, for the Lord will certainly make a lasting dynasty for my master, because he fights the Lord's battles. Let no wrongdoing be found in you as long as you live."*[25]

She applauds David for the good services he had done against the common enemies of their country, the glories of which, she hopes, he will not stain by any personal revenge toward Nabal. *"... [He] fights the Lord's battles ..."*[26] against the Philistines, and therefore she implores David to leave it to God to fight his battles against those that affront him. She says, *"Let no wrongdoing be found in you as long as you live."*[27] The King James Version says it like this: *"Evil has not been found in thee all thy days."* In other words, David, you have not done wrong to any of your countrymen even though Saul has been persecuting you as a traitor. And David, I don't believe you're going to start now. She was generous, magnanimous, and effusive in her praise of David; it was not, however, false praise under false pretenses just to get her husband out of trouble. She spoke the truth.

A peacemaker depends upon God's grace.

"Now since the Lord has kept you, my master, from bloodshed and from avenging yourself with your own hands, as surely as the Lord lives and as you live, may your enemies and all who intend to harm my master be like Nabal."[28]

Abigail takes it for granted that she has gained her point already, perhaps perceiving by David's countenance, that he was beginning to change his mind. She depends, not upon her own reasoning, but upon God's grace to appease him, trusting it to accomplish a powerful work in his heart.

She intimates that it was below David to take vengeance on so weak and impotent a man as Nabal when she says, *"May your enemies and all who intend to harm my master be like Nabal."*[29]

Abigail trusts that God's grace will do its work by reminding David of what he was about to do: shed blood and avenge himself, when in fact, it was not even him who was personally affronted. She continues, *"Now since the Lord has kept you, my master, from blood shed and from avenging yourself with your own hands ..."* These words were enough to work upon the gracious spirit which David possessed. We see in a later verse that her words had their intended effect.

A peacemaker helps people see both sides of an issue.

"When the Lord has done for my master every good thing he promised concerning him and has appointed him leader over Israel, my master will not have on his conscience the staggering burden of needless bloodshed or of having avenged himself. And when the Lord has brought my master success, remember your servant."[30]

She is encouraging David by helping him consider both sides of the issue. She seems to remind David that it will be much better for him in the long run, since he is one day going to reign over Israel, that it is best not to have blood from this encounter on his hands and conscience. She reserves this argument for the last, and it is a very powerful one with as good a man as David. She reminds him that the less he indulges his revengeful passion now, the more he can live with a clear conscience later.

Abigail cannot but think that if David should avenge himself in the present, it would be something for which he would be sorry for the rest of his life. So many times we, in the heat of the moment, do things which we have a thousand times wished we had not done. The sweetness of revenge soon turns into an acrid bitterness.

Abigail is confident that if David lets this slide and chooses not to kill Nabal, he will afterwards not only be happy he didn't do it, he would have the unspeakable satisfaction that his wisdom—and God's grace—had gotten the better of his passion.

When we are tempted to sin, whether in word, action, or thought, we should consider how it will appear in the future. Learn from Abigail's wisdom toward David that we should not do anything that we will later in life come to deeply regret. As a wise person once said, "It is better to sleep on what you plan to do than to be kept awake by what you've done."

A peacemaker gains respect and gratitude.

David had time to listen and consider Abigail's arguments. He turned to her and said, *"Praise be to the Lord, the God of Israel, who has sent you today to meet me."*[31] David gives God thanks for sending him this ravishing roadblock, impeding his way on the path of regret.

When a friend brings help and kindness to us, whether it is spiritual, physical, or emotional, we should always give thanks to God. When a friend speaks counsel, direction, comfort, caution, or reproof—a right word at the right time—we must view these words as coming from God. We ought to be very thankful for those happy hindrances which are means of preventing sin in our lives.

By doing this, Abigail causes David to give praise to God, and this thereby gains her respect and gratitude.

A peacemaker is blessed.

David heaps praise and thanks on Abigail for standing between him and a major blunder in his life. *"May you be blessed for your good judgment and for keeping me from bloodshed this day and from avenging myself with my own hands."*[32]

Most people think it's enough to receive a reproof with patience and humility; there are few, however, who will receive it thankfully, commending the one who gave it. Due to her sagacity and humility, Abigail was not only instrumental in saving her foolish husband and possibly her family from death, she was also instrumental in saving David and his men from sin and its long-lasting repercussions. A Japanese proverb says, "The reputation of a thousand years may be determined by the conduct of one hour." David blessed Abigail because of her actions. His reputation for years to come was intact.

Action Steps for a Peacemaker

We can talk a lot about the importance of peacemaking, but until we put peace into practice, it's just words. Here are four suggested action steps you can take to put you on the road to becoming a peacemaker.

Make sure you're at peace with God.

Begin here. If you have not yet put your faith in Christ alone for your salvation, the Bible says that you are at war with God. *"His purpose was to create in Himself one new man out of the two, thus making peace; and in this one body, to reconcile both of them to God through the cross, by which He put to death their hostility."*[33]

It's time to have a peace conference with the Prince of Peace. There is no way to have the peace of God until you know the God of peace.

Years ago, British admiral Lord Horatio Nelson, won a battle at sea against the French. The French Admiral came before him to surrender. He was dressed in full naval regalia, with medals pinned to his chest, his glittering ceremonial sword dangling by his side. He reached out his hand to Lord Nelson as if they were now friends. Lord Nelson stepped back and said, "Your sword first."

You can't just walk up and shake the hand of Jesus without laying down your sword. You must surrender. I like what seminary president Haddon Robinson said: *"No peace will exist between nations until peace reigns in each country. And no country will have peace unless peace resides in each community. And no community will have peace unless peace dwells within its people. And no people will have peace unless they surrender to the Prince of Peace."*

Lead others to be at peace with God.

Ephesians says that your *"desire to tell the good news about peace should be like shoes on your feet."*[34] 2 Corinthians 5:18 says that we have been given the ministry of reconciliation as if God were making His appeal through us to others. As Christ-followers, it is our responsibility to share the Good News of the Gospel everywhere we go, and with everyone we meet. As we do this, we can be used by God in bringing others into a right relationship with Him—a relationship of peace. There is no higher calling—nothing which can bring greater satisfaction—than leading someone to being at peace with God. *Be at peace with those around you by removing a judgmental spirit from your heart.*

Jesus Himself tells us, *"Do not judge others, and God will not judge you; do not condemn others, and God will not condemn you; forgive others, and God will forgive you."*[36]

Do you need to make things right with someone today? Is there anyone you need to forgive? Do you need to ask for forgiveness from someone?

Don't act like one of the *Peanuts* comic strip characters. Lucy said to Charlie Brown, *"I hate everything and I hate everybody, and I hate the whole wide world."* Charlie responded, *"I thought you had inner peace."* To which Lucy replied, *"I do, but I have outer obnoxiousness."*

Do you recall how much David wanted to slay Nabal for the perceived slight David received from him? This is a basic principle. Have you ever noticed it in your own life? If you return evil for evil, it puts you on the same level as the person who did you evil. If I am to be a representative of Jesus Christ, and He says I am to love my neighbor because He loves my neighbor, then I am to have a totally different standard of conduct from the world around me.

Only God understands the motivation of the one who causes us pain. You and I have no idea of the circumstances leading to what someone might have done to us. Only God is able to judge and to give adequate retribution, if necessary. Judgment is the work of God.

Help others who are in conflict.

How can God use you to build bridges between people who are in conflict? Peace is hard to make and even harder to keep. It's usually easier to walk away from a problem instead of getting involved in someone else's difficulty. Be like Francis of Assisi, who prayed, *"Lord, make me an instrument of your peace. Where there is hatred, let me sow love. Where there is injury, pardon."*

Will you say a good word about a person when you hear juicy gossip regarding them? Will you work for peace when there is conflict? Will you seek a solution when you come across an argument? Will you calm the waters instead of stirring them up?

There Are Rewards For Peacemakers

John Adams and Benjamin Franklin worked side-by-side as ambassadors to France in the early days of American nationhood. Once, in 1781, Franklin wrote to Adams, *"'Blessed are the peacemakers is, I suppose, for another world. In this world they are frequently cursed."* While it's extremely difficult to be a peacemaker, there are at least two rewards—two blessings—of which Jesus wants us to be aware.

Blessing #1: You are blessed by God when you make peace.

God applauds and approves those who do what it takes to make peace where there are problems. Martin Lloyd Jones asks the question, *"Why are peace makers blessed? The answer is ... because they are so unlike everyone else ... they are the people who stand out as being different from the rest of the world."*[37]

This beatitude ends with an intriguing phrase, *"... for they will be called sons of God."* The word *called* means to be officially designated as holding a particular rank or office. It is similar to when a chairman is named, a captain is chosen, or a spokesman is designated. It also means to become or to be owned. We could then properly say, "Blessed are the peacemakers, for they shall be owned as the children of God." What Jesus is saying here is that peacemakers will be known and recognized as what they really are—children of God.

Blessing #2: You prove your family connection to God when you make peace.

A peacemaker has the bestowed title of being a child of the Prince of Peace. The phrase *sons of God* refers to a family relationship in which the son takes his father's name and becomes heir to the father's fortune. When the Bible uses the term *son* of someone, that person is *of* their father, and therefore resembles him. It also often bears the meaning, *partaking of the character of.*

Growing up, I loved it when people would say, "You're just like your dad." In fact, that's one of the biggest compliments I can receive to this day, because I love my dad and have always wanted to be as kind, considerate, gentle, and giving as he is.

For years I worked in the construction field when my Dad was the boss. Employees would approach me and ask, "You're Ned Cranston's boy, right?" I'd always smile and say, "Yep, he's my dad." That was a tremendous tribute because evidently people saw something in me that reminded them of my father. Likewise, when you practice and promote peace, a watching world will wonder, *"Is he a son of God? Is she a daughter of God?"* Peacemakers bear a family resemblance and reflect something of the Heavenly Father's character. In his commentary on this passage, William Hendriksen writes, *"It's a designation of high honor and dignity, showing that by promoting peace, they have entered into the very sphere of the Father's own activity. They [peacemakers] are His co-workers."*[38]

When you make peace, you partner with God in spreading peace; you also demonstrate to a watching world that you are a son or a daughter of the King. In addition, you enjoy the full benefits of being in His family. If you want to resemble God, be a peacemaker.

By God's grace, let us apply these principles as a matter of stewardship, realizing that conflict is an assignment, not an accident. We must remember that success in God's eyes is not a matter of specific results, but of faithful, dependent obedience. And let us pray that our service as peacemakers will bring praise to our Lord and lead others to know His infinite love.

Keep your divinity pure. Cleave to the right. Be true to the best in yourself. Fear nothing and regret nothing. Stand boldly for the truth of your testimony. Then, come what may, you will be happy: the whole world cannot cheat you of your conquest.

—*Marcus Aurelius*

Who shall separate us from the love of Christ? Shall trouble or hardship or persecution or famine or nakedness or danger or sword? As it is written: For your sake we face death all day long; we are considered as sheep to be slaughtered. No, in all these things we are more than conquerors through Him who loved us. For I am convinced that neither death nor life, neither angels nor demons, neither the present nor the future, nor any powers, neither height nor depth, nor anything else in all creation, will be able to separate us from the love of God that is in Christ Jesus our Lord.

—*Paul the Apostle*

❖

CHAPTER NINE

The Attitude of Hopefulness

Matthew 5:10-12

When the Messiah preached His message on the mountainside at the beginning of His ministry, He knew what awaited Him; He also knew what was in store for His faithful followers. As we come to the eighth and final beatitude, many of us would like to take a pass on persecution and suffering—me included. Jesus knows, however, that part of following Him means that we will be faced with persecution; therefore, He ends the "Beatitudes" with the following words:

Blessed are those who are persecuted because of righteousness, for theirs is the kingdom of heaven. Blessed are you when people insult you, persecute you and falsely say all kinds of evil against you because of me. Rejoice and be glad, because great is your reward in heaven, for in the same way they persecuted the prophets who were before you.

A pastoral colleague suggests that there are at least six reasons why we can't ignore this beatitude:

1. *It's the last beatitude and serves as a test of all the others. Persecution is as much a normal mark of discipleship as being merciful is.*

2. *It's the longest one because it's the hardest to embrace.*

3. *It's the only beatitude with a command: "Rejoice and be glad."*

4. *It's the only one with an explanation.*

115

5. *It's the only one repeated twice. The word "blessed" is used two times as though Jesus is saying, "You are doubly blessed when you are persecuted."*

6. *It's the only beatitude addressed directly to us. The tense changes from "blessed are those" in verse 10 to "blessed are you" in verse 11.*[1]

In the previous chapter, we focused on the applause that comes from heaven when we do the hard work of making peace in the midst of conflict. It may seem out of place that Jesus would move from peacemaking to persecution and from harmony to hostility. But not all attempts at reconciliation succeed; and no matter how hard we try to make peace with some people, they refuse to live at peace with us.

If we live according to the first seven beatitudes, we will automatically experience the eighth. It's like an equation. If you are the person of the first seven beatitudes you are guaranteed the persecution of the last one. Think about it!

- Embrace the wisdom of being poor in spirit, and some will think you are self-righteous.

- Recognize the importance of mourning over sin, and others will feel convicted and not want you around.

- Discover the joy of meekness, and run the risk of being mistaken as weak and acquiescent.

- Question the acceptance of the spiritual status quo, and instead, hunger and thirst for God; many will label you a religious fanatic.

- Unleash the potential of mercy, and people will call you gullible.

- Release the power of living pure in heart, and feel the tension of a world that lives on lust.

- Encourage the participation of making peace, and get ready for war.

Our faith begins, develops, and matures as we live out the first seven. Our faith is then tested when we come to the last one. Dietrich Bonhoeffer, who wrote a Christian classic entitled, *The Cost of Discipleship*, referred to the "extra-ordinariness" of the Christian life. He asserted, *"With every beatitude the gulf is widened between the disciples and the people, and their call to come forth from the people becomes increasingly manifest."*[2]

What's difficult about this beatitude is that we all like to be liked. Once again, we see that following Jesus is often a paradox. He applauds us when we are in agony and sees great purpose in our persecution. As an interesting side note, those who were listening to Jesus probably had a difficult time with this one. It was a common idea back then that all suffering, including persecution, was an indication that God was not pleased, and that the one who was suffering was somehow to blame for what was happening. This is particularly evident in the Book of Job. Jesus reverses this view. As we take a look at the blessing no one wants, let's observe some truths that Jesus wants us to get our minds and hearts wrapped around.

We Can Expect Persecution

Some of us have bought into the belief that once we have Jesus in our lives, everything will go great. Maybe we've even thought that we should be successful and financially well off. Actually, the Bible says that the exact opposite will happen for those who honor and obey Christ. Jesus never taught the prosperity Gospel, but He did preach a persecution Gospel. Review what Matthew records in verse 10: *"Blessed are those who are persecuted because of righteousness, for theirs is the kingdom of heaven."* The word righteousness refers to living the straight way of following Jesus.

John Stott suggests that we should not be surprised if anti-Christian hostility increases, but rather be surprised if it does not.[3] Jesus said, *"If they persecuted me, they will persecute you also."*[4] Elsewhere He adds, *"The world will make you suffer."*[5] The Augsburg Confession defines the church as the community of those "who are persecuted and martyred for the Gospel's sake." Speaking of their futures, Jesus told the disciples they would face incredible struggles: *"... you will be arrested, persecuted, and killed. You will be hated all over the world because of your allegiance to Me."*[6]

While we can't verify all the facts, church history and tradition tells us that the disciples fared no better than their Leader. *Foxes Book of Martyrs* relates the following:

- James was beheaded. It is said that on his way to be martyred, his accuser was so impressed by his courage and conviction that he repented of his sin, committed himself to Christ, and was then beheaded along with James.

- Phillip was scourged, thrown into prison, and then crucified.

- Matthew was slain with a sword.

- James the Less was stoned to death.

- Matthias was stoned and then beheaded.

- Andrew was crucified and then left hanging on the cross for three days.

- Peter was crucified upside down at his own request because he did not feel worthy enough to be crucified in the same manner as the Lord.

- Jude (Thaddeus) was crucified.

- Bartholomew was beaten with clubs and then crucified.

- Thomas was speared to death.

- Simon the Zealot was crucified.

- John was exiled to an island called Patmos where he died as a prisoner.

Paul, who also lost his life while imprisoned for the faith, mentored young Timothy and asserted, *"And indeed, all who desire to live godly in Christ Jesus will be persecuted."*[7] Another Bible version says it in less formal language: *"Everyone who wants to live as God desires, in Christ Jesus, will be hurt."*[8]

This is echoed elsewhere in the New Testament: *"For it has been granted to you on behalf of Christ not only to believe in Him, but also to suffer for Him."*[9] When Paul wrote to the young church in Thessalonica, he reminded them that Timothy was sent to them, and that *"... the troubles should [not] come as any surprise to you. You've always known that we're in for this kind of thing. It's part of our calling. When we were with you, we made it quite clear that there was trouble ahead. And now that it's happened, you know what it's like."*[10] Peter, after witnessing all that Jesus experienced surmised, *"My friends, do not be surprised at the terrible trouble which now comes to test you. Do not think that something strange is happening to you."*[11] Persecution is to be expected as a normal part of the Christian life.

Why is persecution so pervasive? Simply put, it's due to the nature of Christianity and the sinfulness of human beings. There is such a tension between the message and way of life of Christians and the mindset and way of the world, that conflict is inevitable.

This beatitude tells us that there are two reasons why we will be persecuted:

Because of the Life I Live

Jesus clearly states that His followers will be persecuted *"... because of righteousness."* Some of us might feel mistreated, but it may have nothing do with righteousness. Pastor Ray Pritchard writes, *"If you don't use deodorant, don't claim persecution because no one wants to sit next to you at work. If you're rude to your employees or disrespectful of your boss, don't be surprised to find yourself ostracized."*[12] Some of us believe we're being persecuted for righteous reasons, but it may be because we are self-righteous and are therefore repelling people. Chuck Swindoll writes, *"There are certain reactions we can arouse simply because we adhere to some fanatical extreme that is based on personal or private opinion."*[13] Sooner or later, a sold-out Christ follower will be persecuted due to righteous living. It is an affront to the ungodly; it confronts the will of the world.

Because of the Lord I Love

In verse 11, Jesus says that people will insult, persecute, and say false things, *"... because of Me."* This helps us define the word *righteous.* To be righteous simply means being like the Lord Jesus Christ. For one reason or another, some people are so upset with Jesus that they take it out on those who love Him. Jesus was different, and a world that thrives on conformity cannot tolerate differences.

Those who are following Jesus and are striving to live lives exemplifying His, have a long history of persecution. Think about life in the first-century Christian church.

- Suppose a stone-mason had come to know Christ. Then he was asked to build a temple to a pagan god. What should he do?

- Suppose a seamstress had become a Christian. Then she was asked to make garments for pagan priests. What should she do?

What would you do? What's your call? Whatever you chose, they refused. Are we far too willing to compromise?

The early Christians knew where their loyalty should be. Approximately 100 years after the beginning of the church, a man came to Tertullian, one of the church fathers, with a business problem. After he shared his difficulties, explaining to Tertullian that if he came down on the side of righteousness, it might well cost him his life, he asked, "What can I do? I must live!" The godly church leader replied, "Must you?" We, like Tertullian, should know that the primary concern of the Christian is not living but following Christ.

Likewise, following Christ made a real difference in the early Christian's social life. Most feasts were held in the temple of a god. Even a meal in an ordinary house began with a cup of wine poured out in honor of the gods. Should a Christian share in that? The answer was clear to the early saints. Believers had to cut themselves off from certain types of practices and, consequently, from some people in their lives.

Following Christ impacted the home lives of many first-century believers. Often father, mother, brother, and sister would shut out the child or sibling who made a commitment to Christ. Following Christ during that time could bring the gravest of all consequences. Many Christians forfeited their very lives rather than compromise their Christianity. In Jesus' day, Rome ruled the world. The Emperor came to be regarded as a god. Every year a person had to burn a pinch of incense in honor of Caesar and say, "Caesar is lord." It was simply a test of political loyalty. After the person burned the pinch of incense and received a certificate called a libellus, which declared the offering to Caesar had been rendered, the person could then worship any god he or she chose. Many Christians refused to engage in this practice. Thousands were tortured and killed because of their unflagging devotion to Christ.

In light of what Christians of previous generations have endured, Jesus' words come to us today; and our Lord tells us that you and I may be on the receiving end of:

Verbal Insults

The word "insult" means to chide, taunt, or defame. In another Gospel Jesus addressed this: *"Blessed are you when men hate you, when they exclude you, and insult you, and reject your name as evil, because of the son of man."*[14] Biblically speaking, to be insulted speaks of misrepresentations that degrade another's reputation; it is closely related to slander. This often takes the form of verbal abuse and insulting language. For example, the early church was accused of cannibalism as it gathered to observe the Lord's Supper. This also happened to Christ while He was on the cross. People *"shouted abuse"* at Jesus, *"shaking their heads in mockery"* as they passed by the cross.[15] When you are insulted for believing in the Son of God and the Word of God, you're on the right track!

Or, we might undergo ...

Physical Attack

The word *persecute* can be defined as chasing away someone or something; it also carries the meaning of pursuing someone with a hostile intent; it has the idea of being hunted down like an animal. It can also be defined as repeatedly raiding another's life or property, or to continually annoy someone in a threatening manner.

Pastor Bill Prater described the persecutions that Christians have faced in these words:

> *All the world knows of the Christians who were flung to the lions or burned at the stake, but these were kindly deaths. Nero wrapped the Christians in pitch and set them alight and used them as living torches to light his gardens. He sewed them into skins of wild animals and set his hunting dogs upon them to tear them to death. They were tortured on the rack; they were scraped with pincers; molten lead was poured hissing upon them ... eyes were torn out; parts of their bodies were cut off and roasted before their eyes; their*

hands and feet were burned while cold water was poured over them to lengthen the agony. These things are not pleasant to think about, but these are the things a man had to be prepared for, if he took his stand with Christ.[16]

The persecution of which Jesus spoke may also mean we will face ...

False Accusations

After verbal assaults and physical attack, followers of Christ will also face those who *"falsely say all kinds of evil ..."* You've probably been on the receiving end of some false and hurtful statements; it certainly doesn't minister to your spirit! The psalmist understood this and cried out, *"Malicious people bring charges against me. They ask me things I know nothing about."*[17]

Jesus faced false charges as well, and according to Peter's first epistle, *"He did not retaliate."*[18] Some people like to say things behind our backs, but remember: they did the same to Jesus as His enemies tried to destroy His good name.

We Are to View Persecution as a Gift

Most of us can agree that persecution is a given, but to say that it is a gift is a stretch for us. We are blessed when people mess with us because of our faith: the kingdom of heaven is our reward! No one can take that away. Before Stephen was stoned to death, Dr. Luke relates that he *"only had eyes for God, whom he saw in all His glory with Jesus standing at His side."*[19]

The writer of Hebrews described what happened to a number of the heroes of our faith: *"Others were made fun of and beaten with whips, and some were chained in jail. Still others were stoned to death or sawed in two or killed with swords. Some had nothing but sheepskins or goatskins to wear. They were poor, mistreated, and tortured."*[20]

As the text continues, it presents a rather curious phrase: *"The world did not deserve these good people ..."*[21] This world was not their home; in some mysterious way, they saw persecution as a gift that brought them to their heavenly home.

When Dietrich Bonhoeffer left a Nazi prison on his way to the gallows just days before the Allies freed the camp in which he was detained, he reportedly said, *"This is the end—for me, the beginning of life."* He understood that those who are persecuted for Christ's sake inherit the kingdom of Heaven.

God approves those who face the antagonism of those opposed to His Son. Persecution is the trigger that causes God to pour out His blessings on your life. The martyred missionary Jim Elliot said, *"He is no fool who gives what he cannot keep in order to gain what he cannot lose."* He comprehended, by faith, that there is something more than just what we can physically see in this life. For the persecuted believer, the best is yet to come.

Persecution Brings at Least Two Things to My Life: Joy and Gladness

As Jesus continues this beatitude, it becomes increasingly mind-boggling: *"Rejoice and be glad, because great is your reward in heaven, for in the same way they persecuted the prophets who were before you."* We generally rejoice when we get good news: the baby was born, the anticipated promotion was given, the Christmas bonus was received, or the kids brought home good report cards. The phrase *be glad* is a command, meaning to leap with exuberant gladness or to jump with exceeding excitement.

Luke recorded the Beatitudes of Jesus in chapter six of his Gospel narrative. Jesus says, *"Blessed are you when men hate you, when they exclude you and insult you and reject your name as evil, because of the Son of Man...."* He goes on to say that our reaction should be to *"leap for joy because great is your reward in heaven."*[22] Jesus is not implying that we should be happy about persecution itself. We are to leap for joy for what persecution represents. Let me suggest four reasons why we should rejoice when persecuted:

Persecution confirms my relationship with Jesus.

Someone has said that persecution is a certificate of Christian authenticity. We should rejoice that people see Jesus in us. Peter exhorts us in the following: *"If you suffer as a Christian, do not be ashamed, but praise God that you bear that Name."*[23] Jesus thinks enough of you to let you share in some of what He went through. In the Acts of the Apostles, we learn that after the apostles were put in jail for preaching the Gospel, they were brought before the Sanhedrin to answer the charges against them. Peter gave a biblical and impassioned testimony about Jesus Christ and the Gospel they had been jailed for proclaiming. This made some of the Sanhedrin so furious they demanded the apostles be put to death.[24] The speeches of Peter and the other apostles, along with cooler heads, prevailed that day. Luke then records, *"The apostles left the Sanhedrin, rejoicing because they had been counted worthy of suffering disgrace for the Name."*[25] Persecution and suffering is the badge of authentic discipleship; it confirms that I am His and He is mine.

Persecution causes me to rely on Jesus.

When we suffer, we are more prone to self-examination and are therefore forced to lean on God in ways that we have never done before; when we do, we see God's power. Paul experienced this: *"I am very happy to brag about my weaknesses. Then Christ's power can live in me. For this reason I am happy when I have weaknesses, insults, hard times, sufferings, and all kinds of troubles for Christ. Because when I am weak, then I am truly strong."*[26]

Persecution cultivates righteousness in my life.

One of the best ways to grow is to go through some grief. Peter contends, *"In His kindness God called you to His eternal glory by means of Jesus Christ. After you have suffered a little while, He will restore, support, and strengthen you, and He will place you on a firm foundation.*"[27] That's why Jesus mentions the persecution the prophets faced before us. They serve as models because their rejection was the rule, not the exception. To suffer for what is right is to be part of a great succession of godly men and women. Go often to these great men and women of old and get inside their hearts. Put yourself on the rack with them and learn how to love heaven with them.

Persecution confers a reward.

Jesus said that we should *"rejoice and be glad."* What an incredible statement! It should be obvious that Jesus was not implying that persecution itself makes us happy. Persecution is difficult. It is hard. Persecution hurts. Jesus was not declaring that we should rejoice because of the persecution. Rather, He was saying that we should rejoice and be glad, *"for your reward in heaven is great."* We rejoice because of our reward.

Imagine that you receive a phone call from out of the blue. On the other end of the line, someone announces that you have won one hundred dollars. You might look over at your spouse and with a smile say, "Honey, I've got some good news. We've just won a hundred dollars. I'm glad, aren't you?" But if the phone rang again, and the person said that there had been a mistake—that instead of winning a hundred dollars, you had won a hundred million tax-free dollars. How would you respond then? What would you do? Certainly, this piece of news would call for an entirely higher level of gladness, don't you think? Instead of looking over at your couch-potato spouse with a smile, you might well leap to your feet—even leap around the room a few times. Your spouse may have to tackle you in order to find out why you are so excited. There are different levels of gladness.

This gives us an idea of what Jesus was speaking of when He said that our reward in heaven would be great. He means that those who are persecuted for the sake of righteousness have a reward that is worth leaping and shouting about.

Sometimes when we're suffering, all we can do is focus on the reason for our suffering—on the act of suffering itself. But Jesus said even in the midst of the suffering, we can jump for joy because of what's ahead.

Toward the end of his life, the apostle Paul had every confidence that God would release him from his difficulties. He wrote the following to Timothy from his prison cell: *"The Lord will rescue me from every evil attack ..."* But, recognizing that God may have other plans, the verse concludes: *"... and will bring me safely to His heavenly kingdom."*[28] This promise gave Rowland Taylor, Bishop Ridley, and John Bradford the impulse to kiss the stakes at which they were burned. After receiving countless lashes that turned his back to jelly for Jesus, Obadiah Holmes said, *"You have struck me with roses."*

The Beatitudes are not easy to live. Perhaps that's our problem. We've made the Christian life way too painless. We've gone along and gotten along. Let me ask you a few questions:

- *What have you done in the last month that has caused anyone to challenge your faith?*

- *When have you risked speaking out for Jesus? How have you defended the cause of Christ?*

- *Have you identified yourself to anyone lately as a Christ follower?*

Maybe you've not said anything against Jesus; you really haven't said anything at all. Perhaps you're not sensing any persecution because people don't see the Savior in your life.

Every Christian who puts Christ first will face flak somehow, somewhere, at some time.

- Have you been made fun of for your faith?

- Perhaps you're just ignored because someone thinks you're too religious.

- That promotion at work may be elusive because of your principles.

- You may feel judged and condemned by family members.

- Maybe you face sarcasm from a spouse who does not share your faith.

Remember, persecution is a *given*. It's a *gift* that comes with blessings. And it should bring us joy and gladness because the rewards are worth the risk.

In the early days of the church, a Christian offended the king and was threatened with banishment because of his preaching. He replied, *"Sire, you cannot banish me, for the world is my Father's house."* The king then said he would confiscate all his possessions. The Christian answered, *"Sire, you cannot confiscate my possessions because my treasures are laid up in heaven."*

The king was becoming furious and told the preacher that he would make him live in isolation away from all his friends. The preacher stated, *"Sire, you cannot remove me from my greatest friend, because He lives within me."* Finally the king shouted out, *"Then I'll have you killed!"* To which the Christian calmly replied, *"You can take my breath, but you can never take my life for it is hid with God in Christ."* That's someone who understood that persecution will come, but who also remembered that it would usher him into the joy and gladness of God.

In his book, *The Heavenly Octave*, author Frank Boreham ends his chapter entitled "The Martyr's Crown" with these stirring thoughts. We shall end ours here as well:

> *So true it is that the blood of the martyrs is the seed of the Church. And not only so. It is the constant and abiding inspiration of the Church. Here, for instance, is a young*

man. In the hour of temptation, he yields a sacred principle. He suddenly remembers that for the same principle his forefathers bled; and, blushing, he recoils from the allurement and plays the man. Here is a young woman. She was inclined to forsake the courts of the Lord's house, and her face was only occasionally seen in the sanctuary. She remembers that, in order to secure to her the inestimable privilege of worshiping God according to her conscience, the noblest spirits of all time laid down their lives by the score; and, as a consequence of that reflection, the congregation sees her oftener now.

> Speak, History! Who are life's victors?
> Unroll thy long annals and say-
> Are they those whom the world calls the victors
> who won the success of a day?
> The Martyrs or Nero—the Spartans
> who fell at Thermopylae's tryst,
> Or the Persians and Xerxes?—his judges or Socrates—
> Pilate or Christ?

To that question there can be but one answer. History and experience agree in giving it. And, in giving it, they can find no language better suited to their purpose than the language of the eighth beatitude."[29]

Discussion Questions for Personal or Group Study

Chapter One

1. After reading what James has to say about our attentiveness and obedience to the Word of God, what areas come to mind in your own life that might hold opportunities for growth?

2. How would *you* define humility, and why do you think that this particular quality is mentioned so many times in Scripture?

3. Challenge yourself this week to be consistent with your quiet times and set clear goals, the attaining of which (or striving for) will make you more like Christ. Which of the qualities discussed in this chapter stand out in your mind as a good place to get started?

4. What were some of your New Year's resolutions this year, and how would you change or amend your list after considering your decisions in light of eternity?

5. After reading this chapter, has your perspective on your responsibility as a believer changed at all? If so, how has it changed?

6. The "let's pretend" story from Chuck Swindoll places great emphasis, as does James, on action. "Do" something about what you hear, read, meditate on and memorize. Taking an honest measure of your own life, can you picture yourself as one of the employees left behind, or would your employer return to find his business running smoothly, just as he directed?

Chapter Two

1. Taking into consideration the dual meanings of the word "poor" in the Greek language, the complex idea of the word in Hebrew, and Barclay's paraphrase based on these meanings, what new insight have you gained into the beatitude, "Blessed are the poor in spirit?"

2. If you are ready to take steps toward claiming the blessing promised by our Lord in this first beatitude, pray the following aloud as a verbal commitment:

   Lord, first I acknowledge that I have been born in an impoverished condition, deserving nothing save the righteous judgment of a holy God. I come to you in humility, asking that you teach me to put others ahead of myself, to look only to you for my salvation, and to spend time in the valley of humility, learning that to be nothing next to you is a freeing truth; that I was designed to praise and honor you and not myself, and to find sweet release and blessing in such expressions of truth and praise.

3. Looking back on recent circumstances, compose a mental list of "black dots" that might have been areas where God was working to humble you. Ask yourself honestly if you have been guilty of focusing on these black dot circumstances and not on the white poster promises and blessings. I urge you to make a commitment today, with God's help, to look at the positive and trust Him in the seemingly negative areas of life, with the knowledge that our God works all things together for good to those who trust Him!

Chapter Three

1. What freedom there is in the knowledge that our tears are not for nothing! Let us praise our Lord that he does not abandon us in times of sadness, but rather comes alongside as our comforter and our teacher! What issue in your life has brought you to tears? Is this an area that has also brought you closer to God? If not, why not take it to Him now?

2. Looking honestly at the sinful condition of your own heart, could you say before God that you have been grieving over the sin that separates you from Him? Are you sorry for your sins, or do you have deep sorrow about your sinfulness? Have you reached the point of mental regret or even emotional remorse, but gone no further? Or, have you reached the point of spiritual repentance required to effect change? Ask God to help you get serious about your sin; repent and turn from your sin so that you can walk in His forgiveness and grace.

3. Looking at the four areas in which God calls us to grieve, which of these areas most easily touch your heart, and which area is least likely to stir your emotions? Have you ever asked God to change your heart in any of these areas, to match your desires and concerns for those of His own heart?

4. The "tsunami of death" comes for 150,000 of our fellow humans every single day, and most of them are "fully unprepared to meet God." How does this realization affect or change your perspective concerning your role in world evangelization? Does it give you a sense of urgency—urgency in your prayers as well as your actions? How can you be Christ's "witness" more effectively? How can you care for others more tangibly? How can you pray more urgently? Spend time asking God these questions and journaling the answers, then make an action plan and ask someone to keep you accountable to it.

Chapter Four

1. Briefly summarize how you defined meekness prior to this study, and summarize your impression of the definition now, based on what you have read.

2. "A meek person refrains from revenge and leaves vindication with God." Which Bible characters' lives do you think best portray this lesson (either by leaving things in God's hands or by attempting to take their own revenge and suffering the consequences), and what can we learn from their example(s)?

3. Which of these challenges, inspired by the illustrations in Chapter Four, will you choose to practice this week in your daily life and relationships?

    a. "The meek know what it is to live under the rule and reign of Jesus Christ." Allow the Spirit of God to control you rather than relying on self control—a meekness makeover, if you will.

    b. Following the example of Professor Blackie, who in your life needs your meekness to lead them closer to Christ? Beginning with the first person that comes to mind, construct a simple, yet specific plan that will enable you to go out of your way to care for them in a Christ-like way.

    c. Like Moses experienced with Aaron and Miriam, has anyone questioned your abilities or wondered whether or not you were the right person for the job? Have you considered "throwing quills" at them? Wouldn't it be better to rely on God for vindication? Sharing your experiences can encourage others; let's take this opportunity to discuss our own stories.

4. Prayer: *May I abandon myself to Christ, accept the word of God, attach myself to the Spirit of God, associate with the people of God, and address myself to God's mission, both for this world and the next. Amen.*

Chapter Five

1. How are the words "hunger" and "thirst" used differently in the Beatitudes than in all other Scripture references?

2. Why do you think Jesus chose these words to describe how we should seek righteousness?

3. Have you been a spiritual junk food addict? In what way? What should you be doing differently? What will you commit to doing differently?

4. List a few "wrong" ways to seek righteousness, and then describe the three elements of the righteousness that Jesus tells us to hunger and thirst after.

5. Are you ready to commit to the following principles? If so, take this opportunity to ask God to grant you the grace and help you to keep your resolve and stay on the path to desperately seeking and desiring righteous.

   • When I am spiritually hungry and thirsty, I will pursue holiness more than happiness.

   • Specifically, I will pursue a holy life, holy speech and a holy disposition.

   • When I am spiritually hungry and thirsty, I will be obedient to God.

   • When I am spiritually hungry and thirsty, I will avoid spiritual indifference.

Chapter Six

1. What is the difference in distinction and purpose of the second four commands in the beatitudes when compared to the first four?

2. Define mercy—both as a concept and what it looks like when it is put into practice.

3. Why is mercy an even greater blessing to the one who grants it than it is to the recipient?

4. "Mercy that is action ministers to others." How can we, as believers, demonstrate Christ's mercy towards us in our daily lives with those we come into contact with? Be specific.

5. Who needs your forgiveness, but does not deserve it? What downtrodden person can you serve? Ask God to bring these people across your path this week, and ask also that you may have the grace to grant mercy to others, even as God has granted mercy to you.

6. Journal Opportunity: First, list the four dimensions of mercy, and then under each of these four dimensions, determine a tangible goal that you can strive to reach in the coming weeks and months of your life. If you need help getting started, consider this: Start with the need that is near you.

Chapter Seven

1. Thinking back to your childhood, which character most inspired your dress-up or Halloween costumes? (Jeff's was Batman!) Why?

2. Being completely honest, can you think of any "masks" you might be wearing around other people? What are you trying to hide by wearing this mask? Around whom do you wear it?

3. What character qualities or attributes does a person who is pure in heart possess? Which of these qualities might be lacking in your life? Which do you think is the most important quality?

4. What are the three benefits of being pure in heart, as listed in this chapter?

5. King David was known as a "man after God's own heart," and yet the Scripture tells us that he committed the acts of adultery and murder. What can we learn from David's example about our relationship with God? If you have harbored any hidden sin in your life, take this opportunity to repent and read through the words of David in Psalm 51.

6. Prayer: *Oh, Lord, create in me a clean heart and renew a right spirit within me. I ask that you continue to work in my life to make me more like You each day. I want to be a man/woman after your own heart. I want my character to be free from disguises and wrong motives—I want to be pure of heart! Thank you for the example of David that shows me that to become like you, I do not have to be perfect; I need only sincerely repent of my sin and You will cleanse me and restore me to relationship with You. Amen.*

Chapter Eight

1. In your own words, describe why Abigail's speech and gifts to David and his men were so effective. What peacemaking traits (or strategies) might we learn from her?

2. What are the four action steps that you can take to put you on the road to becoming a Christ-like peacemaker?

3. What are the blessings, listed in the chapter, in store for a peacemaker?

4. Challenge: It is an unfortunate truth that we often face conflict in our relationships with others, even fellow believers. Proverbs 15:1 says, "A gentle answer turns away wrath, but a harsh word stirs up anger." Using this verse as a guide, conduct a "peacemaking experiment" this week. Act as a peacemaker in all of your interpersonal relationships by having a kind response regardless of the way someone addresses you.

Chapter Nine

1. How do you feel about these eight commands with blessings, considering that Jesus knew what harm would befall himself and his disciples prior to giving his "mountainside message" now known as the Beatitudes?

2. After reading the six reasons we can't ignore this final beatitude which of them stands out to you as the strongest argument, and which as the most difficult to accept?

3. How can we be sure that the persecution we suffer is due to righteousness and not self-righteousness (or some extreme personal opinions, etc.)?

4. In what ways were the members of the early church prone to persecution? In what ways are you likely to be persecuted?

5. For what reasons can we, as believers, rejoice in the face of suffering?

6. Challenge: "The primary concern of the disciple is not living, but following Christ." Jesus told the disciples they would face incredible struggles: "... *you will be arrested, persecuted, and killed. You will be hated all over the world because of your allegiance to Me.*" These very words assure us that it isn't safe to follow Jesus. Will you do it anyway?

Bibliography

Barclay, William, *The Gospel of Matthew, Vol. 1.* Philadelphia: The Westminster Press, 1958.

Barclay, William, *The Gospel of Matthew, Vol. 2.* Philadelphia: The Westminster Press, 1958.

Boreham, F. W., *A Temple of Topaz,* London: The Epworth Press, 1928.

Boreham, F. W., *Dreams at Sunset,* London: The Epworth Press. 1954.

Boreham, F. W., *The Heavenly Octave,* Grand Rapids, MI: Baker Book House, 1936.

Bowan, Marjorie, *The Life of John Knox,* London: Watts & Co., 1940.

Campbell, Donald, *Daniel, Decoder of Dreams,* Wheaton, IL: Victor Books, n.d.

Colson, Charles, *The Body,* Dallas, TX: Word Publishing, 1992.

Guiterman, Arthur, *Gaily the Troubadour,* New York: Dutton, 1936.

Hasler, Richard A., *Journey With David Brainerd,* Downers Grove, IL: InterVarsity Press, 1975.

Hendriksen, William, *Exposition of the Gospel According to Matthew,* Grand Rapids: Baker Book House, 1973.

Henry, Matthew, *The Pocket Bible Commentary: Volume 7: Matthew-Luke,* Chicago: Moody Press, n.d.

International Standard Bible Encyclopedia, Vol. 4: Q-Z. Geoffrey W. Bromiley, Editor. Eerdmans, 1988.

Lattimer, Jule-Ann, *The Quiet Hour,* December, 1997-February, 1998.

Lewis, C. S. & Clyde S. Kilby, (Editors) *Letters to an American*

Lady, Grand Rapids, MI: William B. Eerdmans, 1967.

Lloyd-Jones, D. Martin, *Studies in the Sermon on the Mount,* Grand Rapids, MI: Eerdman's Publishing, 1959-60.

Maxwell, John, *Thinking For A Change,* New York: Warner Books, 2003.

MacArthur, John, *The MacArthur New Testament Commentary,* Matthew 1-7, Chicago: Moody Press, 1989.

McGowan, Norman, *My Years With Winston Churchill,* London: Souvenir Press, 1958.

Ortberg, John, *Everybody's Normal Till You Get to Know Them,* Grand Rapids, MI: Zondervan, 2003.

Smedes, Lewis B., *The Art of Forgiving: When You Need to Forgive and Don't Know How,* New York: Ballantine Books, Inc., 1996

Stott, John R. W., *Christian Counter-Culture: The Message of the Sermon on the Mount,* Downers Grove, IL: InterVarsity Press, 1978.

Swindoll, Charles, *Improving Your Serve,* Dallas, TX: Word Publishing, 1981.

Swindoll, Charles, *Simple Faith,* Dallas, TX: Word Publishing, 1996.

Thigpen, Paul, *Discipleship Journal,* Issue 138, n.d.

Tozer, A. W., *The Pursuit of God,* Harrisburg, PA: Christian Publications, 1982.

Tozer, A. W., *The Root Of The Righteous,* Harrisburg, PA: Christian Publications, 1955.

Notes

Chapter One: Hearing His Voice Today

1. Matthew 5:1-2 (NIV)
2. James 1:19-24 (NIV)
3. James 1:20 (NIV)
4. James 1:21 (NIV)
5. Isaiah 50:5 (NIV)
6. James 1:21b (NIV)
7. Philippians 3:12 (NIV)
8. James 1:22 (NIV)
9. Charles Swindoll, *Improving Your Serve*, Dallas, TX: Word Publishing, 1981.
10. James 1:22 (NASB)
11. James 1:23-24 (NIV)
12. A.W. Tozer, *The Root Of The Righteous*, Harrisburg, PA: Christian Publications, 1955.
13. John Maxwell, *Thinking For a Change*, New York: Warner Books, 2003.
14. James 1:25 (NIV)

Chapter Two: The Attitude of Reception

1. Charles Colson, *The Body*, Dallas, TX: Word Publishing, 1992, p. 124.
2. Acts 3:26 (NIV)
3. Genesis 12:3 (NIV)
4. Malachi 4:6 (NIV)
5. Psalm 4:6 (NIV)
6. Matthew Henry, *The Pocket Bible Commentary: Volume 7 Matthew-Luke*, Chicago: Moody Press.

7. Psalm 10:3 (NLT)

8. Psalm 68:19 (NIV)

9. Isaiah 35:8 (NIV)

10. Psalm 34:6 (NIV)

11. Psalm 35:10 (NIV)

12. Psalm 40:17 (NIV)

13. Psalm 69:32 (NIV)

14. Psalm 70:5 (NIV)

15. Psalm 132:15 (NIV)

16. Ezekiel 28:2 (NASB)

17. Augustus Montague Toplady, *Rock of Ages, Cleft for Me,* The Lutheran Hymnal, St. Louis: Concordia Publishing House, 1941.

18. Luke 18:13 (NIV)

19. Psalm 74:19 (KJV)

Chapter Three: The Attitude of Mourning

1. Proverbs 14:13 (NIV)

2. John R. W. Stott, *Christian Counter-Culture: The Message of the Sermon on the Mount,* Downers Grove, IL: InterVarsity Press, 1978, p. 41.

3. 1 Peter 4:12 (NIV)

4. Psalm 6:6 (NIV)

5. 2 Samuel 18:33 (NIV)

6. Genesis 23:2 (NIV)

7. Ecclesiastes 7:2-4 (NIV)

8. 1 Samuel 1:10, 16 (NIV)

9. Psalm 56:8 (NKJV)

10. Isaiah 53:3-4 (NIV)

11. Romans 7:24 (NIV)

12. Richard A. Hasler, *Journey With David Brainerd*, Downers Grove, IL: InterVarsity Press, 1975.

13. James 4:9 (NIV)

14. Matthew 26:75 (NIV)

15. 2 Corinthians 7:10 (NIV)

16. Psalm 51:3-4 (NIV)

17. Luke 19:41 (NIV)

18. Luke 19:42 (NIV)

19. Marjorie Bowan, *The Life of John Knox*, London: Watts & Co., 1940.

20. Richard A. Hasler, *Journey With David Brainerd*, Downers Grove, IL: InterVarsity Press, 1975.

21. Alan Jackson, *Greatest Hits, Vol. 2*, Arista Records, August 12, 2003.

22. Acts 1:8 (NIV)

23. Romans 6:23 (NIV)

24. 2 Corinthians 5:20 (NIV)

25. John 17:23 (NIV)

26. Romans 10:3 (NIV)

27. Arthur Guiterman, *Gaily the Troubadour*, New York: Dutton, 1936.

28. Larry Libby, *Discipleship Journal*, Issue 138, November/ December, 2003.

Chapter Four: The Attitude of Humility

1. Norman McGowan, *My Years With Winston Churchill*, London: Souvenir Press, 1958.

2. Daniel Goleman, *Emotional Intelligence*, Bantan Books. Quoted in Reader's Digest, January, 1996.

3. *The Gospel of Matthew, Vol. 2*, William Barclay, Philadelphia: The Westminster Press, 1958.

4. Donald Campbell, *Daniel, Decoder of Dreams*, Wheaton, IL. Victor Books, p. 22.

5. Matthew 11:29 (KJV)

6. Numbers 12:3 (KJV)

7. Numbers 12:2 (NIV)

8. Ibid.

9. Numbers 12:4 (NASB)

10. John Ortberg, *Everybody's Normal Till You Get to Know Them*, Zondervan, 2003.

11. Genesis 13:8 (NIV)

12. 1 Samuel 24:6 (NIV)

13. Matthew 5:5

14. Matthew 11:28-39 (NIV)

15. A. W. Tozer, *The Pursuit of Gòd*, Harrisburg, PA: Christian Publications, 1982.

16. James 1:21 (NKJV)

17. Galatians 5:22-23

18. Galatians 5:25 (NIV)

19. Ephesians 4:2 (NIV)

20. Ephesians 4:2-3 (NIV)

21. 1 Peter 3:15 (NIV)

Chapter Five: The Attitude of Satisfaction

1. Associated Press, *"New Jersey Woman Downs Six-Pound Burger at Clearfield Pub,"* Lancaster New Era, January 14, 2005.

2. Proverbs 27:7 (NIV)

3. F. W. Boreham, *A Temple of Topaz, Abraham Lincoln's Text*, London: The Epworth Press, 1928. p. 31.

4. Isaiah 55:2-3 (CEV)

5. Luke 15:11-32

6. John 4:13-14 (NIV)

7. John 4:32-34 (NASB)

8. Philippians 3:8 (NLT)

9. Psalm 42:1 (NASB)

10. Psalm 63:1-8 (NIV)

11. Romans 10

12. John MacArthur, *The MacArthur New Testament Commentary*, Matthew 1-7, Chicago: Moody Press, p. 178.

13. Marion Gilbert in *Reminisce*, Reader's Digest, February, 1994, p. 12.

14. Psalm 107:9 (NIV)

15. Jule-Ann Lattimer, *The Quiet Hour*, December, 1997-February, 1998, p. 54.

16. John Brown, quoted in Jerry Bridges, *The Pursuit of Holiness*, Colorado Springs, CO: NavPress, 1978, p. 51.

17. 1 Chronicles 16:29 (NIV)

18. Colossians 1:10-11 (NIV)

19. Colossians 4:6 (NIV)

20. Psalm 19:14 (NIV)

21. Philippians 2:5-8 (NIV)

22. Hebrews 4:15 (NIV)

23. Matthew 11:29 (NIV)

24. Matthew 9:36 (NIV)

25. John 8: 10-11 (NIV)

26. C. S. Lewis & Kilby, Clyde S. (Editor) *Letters to an American Lady*, Grand Rapids, MI: William B. Eerdmans, 1967.

27. 2 Corinthians 7:1b (KJV)

28. Judges 16:20 (NIV)

29. Keith Green, *My Eyes Are Dry*, Album: No Compromise, 1978.

30. Ibid.

31. Deuteronomy 6:5 (NASB)

32. Jeremiah 29:13 (NASB)

33. Matthew 5:6 (NASB)

Chapter Six: The Attitude of Mercy

1. William Barclay, *The Gospel of Matthew, Volume One,* Philadelphia: Westminster Press, 1958, p. 98.

2. Matthew 18:21

3. Matthew 18:22

4. Matthew 18:23-24 (NASB)

5. Matthew 18:26b (NASB)

6. Matthew 18:28 (NASB)

7. Matthew 18:29 (NASB)

8. Matthew 18:30 (NASB)

9. Matthew 18:32-24 (NIV)

10. Lewis B. Smedes, *The Art of Forgiving: When You Need to Forgive and Don't Know How,* New York: Ballantine Books, Inc., 1996.

11. Luke 10:29 (NIV)

12. Luke 10:31-32 (NIV)

13. Luke 10:33 (NIV)

14. Erma Bombeck, "Please, Listen," *Chicago Sun Times,* February 26, 1977.

15. Luke 10:33b (NIV)

16. Luke 10:34 (NASB)

17. Source unknown.

18. Luke 10:37 (NIV)

19. Galatians 6:1 (Msg)

20. Colossians 1:27 (NIV)

21. William Barclay, *The Gospel of Matthew, Volume One,*
    Philadelphia: Westminster Press, 1958, p. 98.

Chapter Seven: The Attitude of Purity

1. Proverbs 23:7 (KJV)

2. Matthew 9:4 (NIV)

3. Proverbs 4:23 (NASB)

4. Genesis 6:5 (NASB)

5. Psalm 51:10 (NASB)

6. Psalm 73:1 (NASB)

7. Jeremiah 17:9-10a (KJV)

8. Matthew 15:19 (NLT)

9. Psalm 24:3-4 (NIV)

10. Exodus 33:18 (NIV)

11. Exodus 33:20 (NIV)

12. Exodus 33:23 (NIV)

13. 1 John 3:2 (NIV)

14. John 14:9 (CEV)

15. Acts 13:22 (NIV)

16. 2 Samuel 11:6-8

17. 2 Samuel 11:11 (NIV)

18. 2 Samuel 11:14-16 (NLT)

19. 2 Samuel 11:27 (NIV)

20. 2 Samuel 12:1-4 (NLT)

21. 2 Samuel 12:7 (NLT)

22. 2 Samuel 12:13 (NLT)

23. Ted Engstrom, *Integrity,* Dallas, TX: Word Publishing,
    1998.

24. Psalm 51 (NIV)

25. Ecclesiastes 3:11 (NIV)

26. Paul Thigpen, *Discipleship Journal,* Issue 138, pp. 64-65.

27. Psalm 119:58 (NIV)

Chapter Eight: The Attitude of Conciliation

1. *Bits & Pieces,* June 25, 1992.

2. Matthew 5:9 (NIV)

3. Matthew 5:9 (Msg)

4. Hebrews 13:20 (NASB)

5. Isaiah 9:6 (NIV)

6. Numbers 6:24-26 (NIV)

7. James 3:18 (NIV)

8. *International Standard Bible Encyclopedia,* Vol. 4:Q-Z, Geoffrey W. Bromiley, Editor. Eerdmans, 1988.

9. Genesis 12:11

10. Genesis 29:17

11. 2 Samuel 13:1, 14:27

12. 1 Kings 1:3

13. Esther 2:7

14. Proverbs 31

15. 1 Samuel 25:18 (NASB)

16. Luke 14:31-32 (NASB)

17. 1 Samuel 25:20 (NIV)

18. Luke 7:44-46 (NIV)

19. 1 Samuel 25:23-24 (NIV)

20. 1 Samuel 25:23b (NASB)

21. 1 Samuel 25:24 (NASB)

22. 1 Samuel 25:18, 27 (NIV)

23. Proverbs 21:14 (NIV)

24. 1 Samuel 25:27 (NIV)

25. 1 Samuel 25:28 (NIV)

26. Ibid. (NIV)

27. Ibid. (NIV)

28. 1 Samuel 25:26 (NIV)

29. 1 Samuel 25:26b (NIV)

30. 1 Samuel 25:30-31 (NIV)

31. 1 Samuel 25:32 (NIV)

32. 1 Samuel 25:33 (NIV)

33. Ephesians 2:15b-16 (NIV)

34. Ephesians 6:15 (CEV)

35. 2 Corinthians 5:18 (NIV)

36. Luke 6:37 (TEV)

37. D. Martin Lloyd-Jones, *Studies in the Sermon on the Mount,* Grand Rapids, MI: Eerdman's Publishing, 1959-60.

38. William Hendriksen, *Exposition of the Gospel According to Matthew,* New Testament Commentary, Grand Rapids: Baker Book House, 1973.

Chapter Nine: The Attitude of Hopefulness

1. Dr. Ray Pritchard, *The Blessing No One Wants,* A sermon preached at Calvary Memorial Church, Oak Park, Illinois, 1996.

2. John R. W. Stott, *Christian Counter-Culture: The Message of the Sermon on the Mount,* Downers Grove, IL: InterVarsity Press, 1978, p. 55.

3. Ibid.

4. John 15:20b (NIV)

5 .John 16:33 (TEV)

6. Matthew 24:9 (NLT)

7. 2 Timothy 3:12 (NASB)

8. Ibid. (NCV)

9. Philippians 1:29

10. 1 Thessalonians 3:3-4 (Msg)

11. 1 Peter 4:12 (NCV)

12. Dr. Ray Pritchard, *The Blessing No One Wants,* A sermon preached at Calvary Memorial Church, Oak Park, Illinois, 1996.

13. Charles Swindoll, *Simple Faith,* Nashville, IN: Thomas Nelson, 2003, p.35

14. Luke 6:22 (NIV)

15. Matthew 27:39 (NLT)

16. Rev. Bill Prater, A sermon preached at Fellowship Baptist Church, Liberal, Kansas, 1998.

17. Psalm 35:11 (GW)

18. 1 Peter 2:23 (NIV)

19. Acts 7:55 (Msg)

20. Hebrews 11:36-37 (CEV)

21. Hebrews 11:38 (CEV)

22. Luke 6:22-23 (NIV)

23. 1Peter 4:16 (NIV)

24. Acts 5:33

25. Acts 5:41 (NIV)

26. 2 Corinthians 12:9-10 (NCV)

27. 1 Peter 5:10 (NLT)

28. 2 Timothy 4:18 (NASB)

29. F. W. Boreham, *The Heavenly Octave,* Grand Rapids, MI: Baker Book House, 1936.

Appendix One

CEV   *Contemporary English Version*
Grand Rapids: Zondervan (1965)

GW   *God's Word Translation*
Grand Rapids: World Publishing, Inc. (1995)

KJV   *King James Version*

Msg   *The Message*
Colorado Springs: NavPress (1993)

NASB   *New American Standard Bible*
Anaheim, CA: Foundation Press (1973)

NCV   *New Century Version*
Dallas: Word Bibles, (1991)

NIV   *New International Version*
Colorado Springs: International Bible Society (1978, 1984)

NJB   *New Jerusalem Bible*
Garden City, NY: Doubleday (1995)

NLT   *New Living Translation*
Wheaton, IL: Tyndale House Publishers (1994)

TEV   *Today's English Version*
New York: American Bible Society (1992)

About the Author:

Dr. Jeff Cranston serves as Lead Pastor of LowCountry Community Church, a multi-campus church in Bluffton and Hilton Head, South Carolina. For over a quarter of a century, his global ministry has included evangelism, leadership development and pastoral training. Jeff is married to Darlene and is the father of three daughters.

Publisher's Note:

Sincere thanks to Laura Zugzda for the cover design and ADI and Stephanie Martindale for layout.

Further information about the life and work of F. W. Boreham is available at the F. W. Boreham Facebook page:

http://www.facebook.com/pages/F-W-Boreham/121475236386

and The Official F. W. Boreham Blog Site:

http://fwboreham.blogspot.com

Your comments and questions are welcome and they can be addressed to:

Michael Dalton
John Broadbanks Publishing
2163 Fern Street, Eureka, CA 95503, USA
dalton.michael@sbcglobal.net

Geoff Pound
c/o HCT, PO Box 4114, FUJAIRAH, United Arab Emirates
geoffpound@gmail.com

Jeff Cranston
LowCountry Community Church
801 Buckwalter Parkway, Bluffton, SC 29910
jcranston@lowcountrycc.org
www.lowcountrycc.org